THE WAY OF ST JAMES

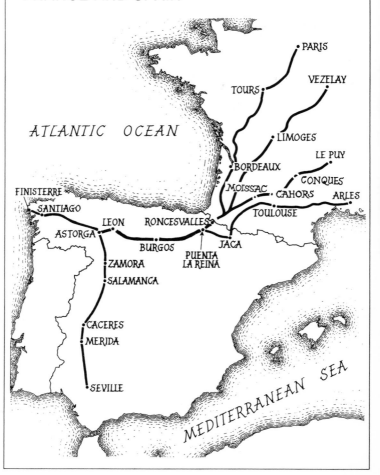

THE MAJOR PILGRIM ROUTES THROUGH FRANCE AND SPAIN

ATLANTIC OCEAN

PARIS

VEZELAY

TOURS

LIMOGES

LE PUY

CONQUES

BORDEAUX

MOISSAC

CAHORS

ARLES

FINISTERRE

SANTIAGO

LEON

RONCESVALLES

TOULOUSE

ASTORGA

BURGOS

JACA

ZAMORA

PUENTA LA REINA

SALAMANCA

CACERES

MERIDA

SEVILLE

MEDITERRANEAN SEA

THE WAY OF ST JAMES
Le Puy to Santiago - A Cyclist's Guide

by
John Higginson

CICERONE PRESS
MILNTHORPE, CUMBRIA

© J. Higginson 1999
ISBN 1 85284 274 1
A catalogue record for this book can be found in the British Library

for
Andrea

Advice to Readers

Readers are advised that whilst every effort is taken by the author to ensure the accuracy of this guidebook, changes can occur which may affect the contents. It is advisable to check locally on transport, accommodation, shops etc but even rights-of-way can be altered.

The publisher would welcome notes of any such changes

Front cover: Burgos (Day 24 & 25)

CONTENTS

Astorga - Plateresque doorway of the Cathedral (Day 29)

INTRODUCTION

In the past ten years a plethora of books and guides has been written about the pilgrimage to Santiago de Compostela. They are all based on a perceived route which (with a few variations each year to circumnavigate building work) has been laid out and clearly way-marked as close to the original pilgrimage route as possible. This route is now walked and ridden along by thousands of pilgrims each year who are constantly making it deeper and wider. The result is that non-walkers tend to find themselves on this pathway. The horse riders manage quite well but cyclists have a number of problems. Those on mountain bikes are able to bounce their way over the boulders and ruts which are to be found everywhere but risk the abuse of walkers who feel (quite justifiably) that their territory is being encroached upon. Touring cyclists find much of it impossible.

As touring cyclists who will never see 50 again, my wife and I realised that if we were to attain our goal of cycling from Le Puy to Santiago, we would have to devise our own route which followed as closely as possible the original way, visiting all the important sites along it, yet avoiding the actual *camino* unless it followed the tarmac.

The following guide is the result of our efforts. It is not perfect nor is it definitive. It is simply our way of achieving our goal by sitting and pedalling and not pushing our bikes along the Way of St James. Our journey was made in July and August of 1997 and was correct at that time. As new roads and accommodation are appearing all the time (and some old ones closing), there may be minor revisions to take into account in subsequent years.

We are not racing cyclists nor are we, even, hardy long distance riders - in fact we found that, most days, 50km was our limit - and so this book has been split into easy daily sections, some shorter than others, to accommodate mountain ranges or difficult roads or fascinating places to visit. It is not prescriptive, however, and those with stronger legs and more courage may wish to split the journey differently. There are some sections of the route which are devoid of accommodation and here there are stages which are longer than they should be. If, in the future, new hotels or hostels are opened, then the length of these sections could easily be re-thought.

The roads used are almost always tarmac. In France they tend to be quiet country lanes and even the short stretches of national roads are not busy and of good quality. Drivers often sound their horns to warn you of their approach, give you a wide berth and a cheery wave as they pass. In Spain there are few country lanes. Most of the roads are wide, fast routes and they usually have a narrow hard shoulder which doubles as a cycle lane. Drivers do not tend to give cyclists much room and heavy lorries often streak down these roads with their near-side wheel straddling the hard shoulder. However, compared with British roads, we found most Spanish ones to be very quiet. In general, the road surfaces were as good as those one finds in Britain but main streets of villages and small towns, particularly in Spain, are often cobbled with deep drains running down the centre. Expect to find farm animals wandering at will on Spanish country roads and in villages expect to find dogs everywhere.

History

St James: James the Great, Jesus' cousin and brother of St John, is as much a character of legend in Spain as St George is in England. Facts about him are hard to come by, but it is fairly certain that he was beheaded by Herod Agrippa in Jerusalem in AD 44 making him the first disciple to be martyred. The rest is merely hypothesis. Reference is made in a Greek text to James having visited Spain on an evangelising mission but, if it did occur, its success was strictly limited. It is then believed that James returned to the Holy Land where he met his fate. It is after James' death that his legend takes wings of fantasy.

His body and head are said to have been taken by Athanasius and Theodore to Jaffa, where a stone boat was commissioned. Within a week, this boat with its precious cargo was washed up at Iria Flavia only 20km from present-day Santiago. The companions were imprisoned but released by angelic intervention and eventually James was buried in a suitable place.

For 800 years, James appears to have lain forgotten and undisturbed, but the hermit Pelagius' vision of a star shining on a field resulted in the discovery of at least one stone tomb and this was confirmed as that of St James. It was not long before Alfonso II, King of the Asturias, had declared him Patron Saint of Spain and soon visions of *Santiago Matamoros* were seen during battles against the Moorish invader, most notably at the battle of Clavijo where he appeared on a white charger to lead the Spanish troops. A church and monastery were built over the tomb and so the history of Santiago de Compostela began. The city's name either originated from *Campus Stellae* referring to the place of the tomb's discovery or *componere* from the Latin, indicating a Roman Necropolis. An interesting recent discovery, however, has confirmed that the interior of one of the tombs does contain an inscription bearing the words, in Greek, 'Athanasius martyr'.

Pilgrimage: People went on pilgrimage for a wide variety of reasons. Many went for personal reasons, to atone for their sins or to profess their faith, others, rather like today's tourists, wanted to visit shrines and venerate holy relics and some even went on behalf of a rich client too busy to go for himself. However, many pilgrims at least began their journey simply to escape the drudgery of their Medieval lives.

The appeal of Santiago de Compostela was manifold. The Holy Sepulchre in Jerusalem had become almost impossible to visit after 1078 when it was captured by the Turks and a pilgrimage to Rome to see the tomb of St Peter meant, for many, a crossing of the Alps with all its attendant hazards. However, the journey to Santiago was a good, long way to travel, it had enough difficulties to make it worthwhile and it had a wealth of shrines and relics to visit on the way. Besides, it was heavily promoted both by the Spanish and by the French Church at Cluny who saw it as a source of future wealth and a way of resisting the threat of Moorish dominance.

As the popularity of the pilgrimage grew (over half a million people per year in the eleventh century) so the number of monasteries, hospitals and hermitages to assist the pilgrims along the way also burgeoned. In the middle of the twelfth century, Aimery Picaud, a monk from central France, produced the first ever guide to the pilgrimage, as part of the *Codex Calixtinus*, which included not only the holy sites but also his unrestrained views on the character and customs of the inhabitants of the regions through which the pilgrim would pass.

The Way to Santiago retained its popularity until the end of the fifteenth century but it never fully declined and, thanks in no small part to the efforts, this century, of the priest of the village of O Cebreiro, Dr. Elias Valiña Sampedro, the pilgrimage is now enjoying a great resurgence. If its popularity continues to grow, especially during the Holy Years (when St James' Day, 25th July, falls on a Sunday), then Santiago may no longer be able to cope with the enormous number of visitors who will descend on it, not just from along the pilgrimage routes but also by air, road and rail.

It is probable that one of the very first pilgrims from Le Puy, Bishop Gottschalk, rode on a horse to Santiago, as did the intrepid Aimery Picaud. Cycling pilgrims, therefore, should not feel inferior to their walking counterparts. They are simply using the mode of transport most suitable for them. There is an apparent hierarchy of pilgrims along the way - walkers look down on cyclists, those who do the whole route look down on those who only cover part of it, those who make the journey under their own steam look down on those who travel its length by car and everyone looks down on the day-trippers who wander around Santiago with their broom-stick staffs and plastic water-gourds - but this attitude should really be discouraged. We are all pilgrims and we should be allowed to make our own pilgrimage in our own way.

Preparation

Bicycles: We received enormous amounts of advice about the bikes we should take on this journey. Many traditionalists told us that the only machine that they would entertain was a lightweight tourer whilst others with a more modern outlook said that nothing but a mountain bike would cope with the terrain we would encounter. In the end we took sound advice and were never to regret it. We had American trail bikes with the strength of a mountain bike but the lightweight versatility of a tourer. They were equipped with gears (42/32/22 drivetrain and 7 speed 11-28) low enough to cope, fully laden, with 1-in-4 hills; highly efficient brakes for the long, vertiginous descents; 'bullet-proof' Kevlar tyres which did not puncture once in 2,600 kilometres; topped off with our own gel saddles for extra comfort. Our only mishap was one broken spoke sustained on the cobbles of a mountain village during a particularly steep descent. We carried spare spokes which are absolutely essential as those on the mainland of Europe are a different size, a spare folding tyre, inner tubes, oil and minimal tools.

Equipment: When we left England on this journey, we expected to be away for anything up to three months and we knew we had to be completely self-sufficient during this time. We also knew that we had to keep the weight on the bikes down to a manageable amount, so we began by making a long list of 'essentials' and then removing anything which was not absolutely essential from it. The result was that we only took one item which we did not use. (The premise, 'If you are not going to use it every day, don't take it' is a good guide apart from emergency equipment.)

When it came to bags, there was only one sensible choice. We only found one manufacturer which guarantees its products totally waterproof and what a difference it makes. Even in torrential thunderstorms and driving sleet, everything inside our panniers and bar bags stayed completely dry without having to be wrapped in polythene bags. Even the rubberised map case atop the bar bag kept out every drop of water although it did turn yellow in the sun of the Meseta!

We did not take a tent and we did not regret it. The extra weight and the effort to erect it at the end of a hard day and to strike camp early each morning is just too much on a journey such as this and the cost of a campsite is very similar to that of a *gîte d'étape*. The only items we took and did not use were self-inflating sleeping mats. They would have been useful if we had been allowed to stay in *refugios* but they are certainly not essential. We took and used lightweight sleeping bags, a change of clothing including padded cycling shorts, Coolmax thermals and socks, Pertex jackets to keep out the wind and waterproof capes. We also took a fibre bath-towel each, a small Gaz stove and basic cutlery and plastic plates. Our luxuries were a camera, mini-binoculars and a Dictaphone.

We had been warned about wild, dangerous dogs along the whole length of the pilgrimage route and, therefore, took a Dog-Dazer - a small, battery-powered instrument which emits a high frequency sound in order to deter dogs from attacking. As we were never called upon to use it, we cannot comment on its efficacy.

Language: Do not expect to find anyone along the whole route who

11

will speak English. This way you will be pleasantly surprised if you do meet anyone who speaks your mother tongue. Along the French section of the route, most of the locals you meet will be from small villages and their French may be difficult to understand at times. In Spain, English is rarely spoken along the *camino* until Santiago is reached. However, many pilgrims do speak English and there will usually be someone on hand who can help you out. It is advisable, nevertheless, to take at least a year's course in both languages before you go and to carry a dictionary of each language for those awkward moments when that special word just will not come. Remember that many of the words and phrases that you will need on this pilgrimage will not be the ones you vaguely remember from school.

Maps and Guides: We tried to keep these down to the minimum because paper weighs so much, but we ended up taking IGN maps No. 50, 57, 58, 63 and 66 for France and Michelin maps No. 441 and 442 of Spain. As soon as we had finished with each we sent it home to reduce the weight. The IGN maps were excellent with only one inaccuracy and covered all but a few kilometres of the journey. The Michelins were not so good. The scale was not fine enough and although they were the latest English editions, we found that they were years out of date with many new roads missing and those which were on the map often had different road numbers in reality. Our only two guidebooks were Alison Raju's *Le Puy to the Pyrenees* and the 1997 Spanish Camino Guide (both from the Confraternity of St James). We had, however, read numerous books and guides before we left home and a list of these can be found in the bibliography.

Full Kit List: Bicycle lights, tools, spare inner tubes, folding spare tyre, puncture repair outfit, plastic tape, water bottles, helmets, cycling gloves, cycle computer, cycle locks, spare spokes, pump and Velcro straps, mending kit.

Dog-Dazer, stove & Gaz, first aid & insect repellent, army knife, scissors, lighter, tissues, polythene bags, pans, cutlery, plates, cups, dishcloth and scourer, universal plug, stretch line, washing-up liquid, clothes-washing liquid and mini cool-bag.

Maps, guides, dictionaries, camera and films, mini-binoculars, Dictaphone, passport, pilgrim passport, E111, currency, credit and debit cards, spectacles and sun-glasses, pen and pencil, notebook and prayerbook.

Toothbrush and gel, shower gel, fibre towels, toilet roll, sun cream, lip salve, clothes, thermals, Pertex jackets, capes, spare shoes, sleeping bags, pocket-pillows and self-inflating sleeping mats, glucose tablets, Isostar sachets, coffee, dried milk and sugar, and an emergency meal (dried soya mince & rice).

Accommodation

On the French portion of the *chemin* most of our nights, with a couple of notable exceptions, were spent in some form of *gîte d'étape*. These had minimum standards including provision of a decent bed, showers and a kitchen. These standards were more often than not exceeded, however, with private rooms, baths, washing machines, fridge / freezers and microwaves. The price varied (in 1997) between 30 and 55 francs per person. In Spain, however, the story was very different. In the high season, most *refugios* (costing up to 1,000 pesetas per person) refused entry to pilgrims on bikes until after 8.00pm because the beds were allocated to walkers who took precedence. In these circumstances we were forced to seek alternative accommodation in small hotels (often called *hostals*, *fondas* or *hospedaje*) or convents. These were fine but stretched our budget to its limit, costing us between 3,000 and 6,500 pesetas per room - be warned! Information about overnight stops is included but should be confirmed by telephone as situations, especially in Spain, change rapidly.

Fitness

We had planned our pilgrimage for two years and were determined to be fit for it. During the winter months we walked four to six miles every day and in the better weather we cycled on three or four days per week, gradually increasing the distance and weight carried. No amount of cycling in Britain, however, can prepare you for the mountains you are going to meet on the *camino*. It is not the steepness of the hills that shocks you but the length. For a single hill, 25km is not unusual with 32km the longeSt Be prepared to spend four hours climbing one major peak. It happened several times. Tiredness can be cumulative and getting on a bike every morning for five weeks and cycling all day in extreme weather conditions is

13

very different from having a hard day out once a week in Britain.

Help Available

Before you leave on this pilgrimage, the best help you can have is from people who have been before. The simplest way to contact these people is through the Confraternity of St James which exists to promote the pilgrimage and help future pilgrims. Do not be afraid to ask what may seem obvious and apparently stupid questions. If you do not ask, you will never know some of the most essential information. Attendance at a 'Practical Pilgrim Seminar' run by the Confraternity would certainly be of great use. These take place twice a year, once in the north of England and once in the south. Everyone starts as a novice and ends an expert - or so we like to think!

Transport

Attempting to reach Le Puy with bicycles can cause problems, as can trying to return from Santiago. It is possible to use the train in France but we found it almost impossible to accompany our bikes and we were not prepared to be separated from them. It is possible to fly with your bike but we heard so many horror stories of bikes being severely damaged in transit that we dismissed this possibility. In Spain, it is now possible to send your bike ahead by road and travel yourself by train but the logistics of this, especially the transport of baggage, made it out of the question. We finally decided to use the excellent services of the European Bike Express, a coach firm which will take you and your bike (which is carried in a large trailer) across France. We travelled to Valence in the Rhône valley and then used a local coach firm (C. Rhodaniens) to take us and our bikes from the Gare Routière in Valence to St Agrève, about 50 miles from Le Puy and we rode the reSt On completion of the pilgrimage we travelled on an ALSA coach with our bikes from Santiago to Bilbao (we could have gone to Irun). It is necessary to book in advance as only two bikes per journey can be accommodated. We then cycled round the Spanish and French coast to Bayonne where we were met by the European Bike Express again and this brought us home. The transport throughout was quick and comfortable and without exception the drivers were helpful and stored our bikes with the utmost care with no resulting damage. The only requests were for us to turn our handlebars through 90 degrees so have an Allen key handy.

The Time to Go

There is no perfect time to make the pilgrimage to Santiago. Everyone will give you a long list of pros and cons for every time of the year but many people, like ourselves, are constrained by outside influences. Travel in winter is virtually impossible because of the difficulties encountered crossing the mountains on passes which are, more often than not, closed. In springtime, the weather will be a little warmer but you can expect snow in the mountains and much of the accommodation may be closed. In summer, expect temperatures of 40°C. across the Meseta and refuges and hotels full of young, Spanish walkers who are using a short portion of the route for a ready-made walking holiday. Autumn sees the temperatures falling and the refuges and hotels less full but you can expect to encounter severe weather at times in the mountains. If I were able to choose the perfect time to make the pilgrimage, I think I would choose a period between mid-May to mid-July and expect to find some extremely cold nights but pleasant day-time temperatures for cycling.

It is essential that you give yourself enough time to make the journey without undue hurry. As it is unlikely that you will do it twice, you should leave sufficient time each day to visit places of interest and still finish your day's ride with some energy left for sightseeing. Walkers tend to leave their overnight halt at first light, but cyclists need not do this as, even in the blistering heat of the Meseta, they create some breeze themselves and can complete a 50km stage comfortably by early afternoon when the sun is at its zenith. We found that the ideal time to find accommodation was about 2.00p.m. when streets were quiet at the beginning of the siesta and many pilgrims were still on the road. If you leave it until late afternoon, you may find yourself being turned away, especially in high season.

Food and Drink

We made it our policy never to carry more than one day's food with

15

us in the form of an emergency meal (dried food). Each day we were able to purchase some form of food - either salad items or a cheap restaurant meal. We had no difficulty in France where, even on Sundays, many food shops are open in the morning. In Spain, it was however often difficult to purchase raw materials and much simpler to buy a ready-made meal in a café or restaurant at a very similar price. Remember, too, that in some areas of Spain, water is turned off between 8.00am and 8.00pm. We always carried two water bottles each and a carton of fruit juice which was readily available everywhere. Bars are found in almost every village along the route in France but are found much less frequently in Spain except in the towns. In Spain, the eating hours are also very different. Many bars and cafés do not open until 10.30am and serve lunch from 2.00pm. Evening meals are often not served until 8.30pm or 9.00pm at the earliest and we found a couple of places where the meal was not served until 11.00pm.

Noise

Finally, a word of warning. As you travel across France, you may be lulled into a quiet bucolic stupor in a land where everyone retires to bed at about 10.00pm and even the church clocks are silenced. Be warned - everything will change the moment you reach Spain. The noise which you will experience will be startling. The different eating hours mean that whole families take to the streets after their evening meal, at midnight, and stay talking (and shouting) to each other for several hours. If you manage to stay in a *refugio*, expect the walkers to be up soon after 5.00am. So, if you want to enjoy a few hours of peaceful, well-earned sleep each night, you are strongly advised to invest in a pair of sturdy ear-plugs!

Using this Guide

As previously mentioned, this guide has been split in 35 daily sections but these are purely arbitrary. Information on places to stay other than those at the end of a day's journey are included so that cyclists may split the route according to their own needs and still have accommodation information.

It cannot be stressed too strongly that a set of IGN maps to cover the French section of the route and Michelin maps, for want of anything better, to cover the Spanish route are essential. The distance to be cycled each day is given in bold type at the beginning of each stage and is accurate to within 5km, depending on the number of 'off the track' places visited each day. When tracing the route on these maps, the words in **bold type** will give the route for the day at a glance. Road numbers were correct at the time of press, but both French and Spanish authorities have a habit of changing them at will. Directions have usually been given to left or right etc. but where there is difficulty a compass direction is also included.

The maps provided which accompany each day's ride are purely schematic and are not all to the same scale. However, they should provide enough visual information to give 'at-a-glance' guidance at awkward junctions etc. The altitude cross-sections which accompany each map should give the cyclist an idea of the terrain to be crossed each day but many small yet stiff climbs simply could not be included for fear of making the cross-section look like a saw blade!

THE ROUTE

Day 1: Le Puy to Monistrol (30km)

Le Puy: *A town to spend time in - visit the Cathedral, the pinnacle church of St Michel d'Aiguilhe, climb inside the Notre Dame de France statue and see the old town with its network of twisting cobbled streets. Have your Pilgrim Passport stamped (with a tampon) in the Cathedral Sacristy. There are many hotels but the greatest welcome will be from the Sisters at the Maison St Francois, Rue St Mayol below Notre Dame de France (Tel. 71.05.96.86). There are restaurants, bars, banks, shops, a bike shop and supermarkets.*

Leave from the Place du Plot. Ride west up the Rue St Jacques, cross the Boulevard St Louis and climb the Rue des Capucins, turn right, then left into the Rue de Compostelle, which becomes the Rue des Pèlerins as it climbs above the town with excellent views of Le Puy and its volcanic rocks. A factory is soon passed on the right. Keep to the tarmac until it meets the wider D589 which undulates and climbs until it reaches a crossroads at **Cordes** (10km). This wide, well-surfaced, quiet road is followed all the way to Monistrol.

Go straight on for another 3km into **Bains** (bar, restaurant, hotel and shop). The road continues to climb to **Montbonnet** (small bar) in 3km. There is a shelter here for lunch. The road now begins to level out followed by a steep descent in wide sweeps to **St Privat d'Allier** which is reached in a further 8km. (Here can be found hotels, shops, restaurants and a campsite. There is also a *gîte* in the old Ecole Chrétien.) The road through the village is narrow and winding.

The final 6km is a steep but exhilarating descent to **Monistrol d'Allier** which straddles the river.

There is a gîte at the Centre d'Acceuil and several good cheap hotels which welcome pilgrims. (Hotel des Gorges, Tel. 04.71.57.24.50. Cycles stored overnight in hotel entrance.) Shops and a restaurant are across the bridge.

Note: This is a short first day for two reasons: first, it allows for a delayed start from Le Puy which often occurs and, second, as well as allowing for a good rest at the end of the first day, it means that you will start the next stage, which begins with the first major hill climb, rested and fresh. If you do feel fit and strong, however, the second day's journey, which is also short, could easily be added to day one.

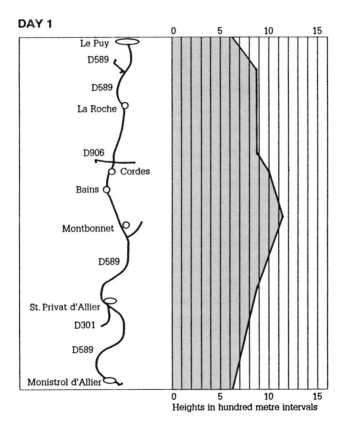

DAY 1

Le Puy
D589
D589
La Roche
D906
Cordes
Bains
Montbonnet
D589
St. Privat d'Allier
D301
D589
Monistrol d'Allier

0   5   10   15

Heights in hundred metre intervals

Day 2: Monistrol to Saugues (16km)

Monistrol: *This small town, dominated by a hydroelectric power plant, is situated in the Allier gorge. Opportunities for white water rafting and canoeing on the river are plentiful as well as walking on a multitude of well-marked paths in woodland which abounds. The church (up a steep hill to the left on far side of bridge) has a carving of a pilgrim on a cross but the entrance may be locked.*

Leave Monistrol by the D589 over the iron river bridge. (Once again you follow this road for the whole of the stage.) Do NOT take the walker's track to the right after the bridge but keep to the tarmac road which, for the first 2.5km, climbs gently in a southerly direction, with the river on your right. Having crossed the river at a right-hand hairpin, the road steepens considerably and climbs above the river in a northerly direction. Ignore the road to the right (to Escluzels) after another 3km and look for a very welcome picnic area further along on the left-hand side of the road. This marks the half-way point of the climb. The whole of this climb is well sheltered by trees and has plenty of opportunities to rest and admire the stunning views of the Allier gorge.

The GR65 strikes off to the left to Montaure and Roziers but there is no need for cyclists to follow this as the track is steep and rough in places and rejoins the D589 just after la **Vachellerie.**

The climb continues without any signs of lessening but when the road turns west for a kilometre, the gradient eases. However, the road is still undulating as it reaches the high plateau of the Gévaudan where it is still common to see shepherds guarding their flocks of sheep and goats. The road continues in a westerly direction for another 5km until a wide valley appears below and to the right, in the centre of which stands your destination, **Saugues**. Sweep steeply right, down into the valley following clear direction signs for Saugues which is reached in a couple of kilometres. The road becomes the town's main street.

Saugues *is an attractive country market town with stone buildings. The church of St Medard is worth a visit, as is the Tour des Anglais, although the latter may be closed. The town contains hotels, restaurants,* *banks, a tourist office, shops and supermarket and a large* gîte d'étape *alongside the stadium beyond the campsite below the town (Tel. 71.77.81.21).*

DAY 2

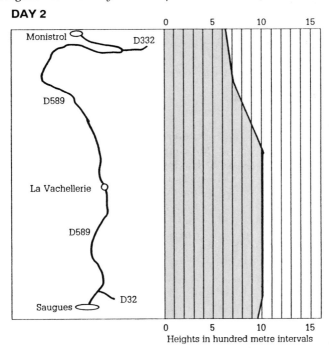

Heights in hundred metre intervals

Day 3: Saugues to Aumont-Aubrac (46km)

Leave **Saugues** in a southerly direction by the D585 with the river on your right. This is an easy straight road which climbs gently until you spy the tower of the *château* at **Esplantas** (bar). Here the road swings sharply right to enter the village via a short, steep hill. Immediately after the village, take the right fork at the T-junction onto the D587. This hilly road through moorland and valley is studded with wild flowers. After travelling 8.5km from the junction, take a right turn into the village of **Chanaleilles**. (Here there is a welcoming bar.)

Continue on the D587 out of Chanaleilles, climbing steeply through woodland interspersed with mountain pasture. In 4km, you will see a track to the left signed 'Le Sauvage' (*gîte d'étape*). Ignore this unless you are desperate for a rest so early in the day and

DAY 3

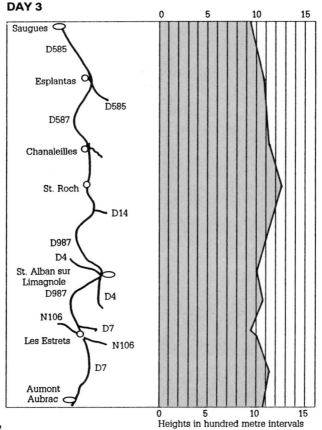

Heights in hundred metre intervals

continue along the D587. In a couple of kilometres the track from Le Sauvage will rejoin the road and soon after, following a long hard climb, the chapel of **St Roch** will be reached.

This grey stone church, which is often locked, has picnic benches outside it and a good shelter alongside if the weather is inclement.

The road numbering now changes and the road you are on becomes the D987, climbing one last ridge before gently descending into **St Alban-sur-Limagnole**.

The town contains hotels, shops and restaurants plus a gîte d'étape above the Hotel du Centre (Tel. 66.31.50.01). The beautiful Romanesque church is worth a visit.

Leave the town in a westerly direction by the D987 for 2km until it crosses the river. Here turn left onto a narrow minor road which climbs steeply to the hamlet of **Chabanes-Planes**. The road now levels out before plunging down to **Les Estrets** where it crosses the N108, turns right and runs parallel to it for 200m, then crosses the **Pont des Estrets** before climbing west again across the high plateau to **Aumont-Aubrac**.

This small market town has hotels, restaurants and excellent small food shops as well as a gîte d'étape run by a hotelier. The Hôtel Prunière (Tel. 04.66.42.80.14) welcomes pilgrims and has secure cycle storage. There is a railway station here and a tourist office in the town hall.

Day 4: Aumont-Aubrac to St Côme d'Olt (60km)

Leave **Aumont-Aubrac** in a westerly direction on the D987 which is followed for the whole day. It is a good, wide, well-surfaced road with little traffic. After 2km, cross the A75 autoroute and climb steadily through woodland for about 6km. With no warning the woodland will come to an end and you will find yourself on the wide open spaces of the Margeride, a strange plateau reminiscent of Dartmoor, which looks as though someone has dumped enormous piles of rock all over it.

Malbouzon (bar) with its wide streets, is the first town of any size to be reached. The next 9km are very exposed across the Margeride but a sharp descent at the end brings you into **Nasbinals**.

Nasbinals is a busy market town with hotels, shops, a market and a gîte d'étape. *A tampon for your Pilgrim Record can be obtained from the priest*

DAY 4

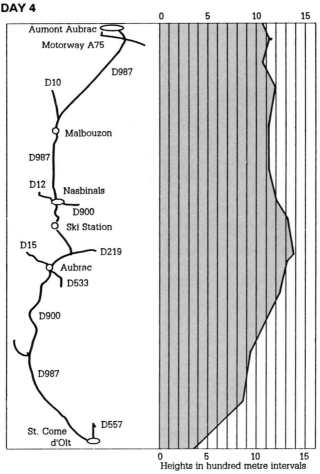

Heights in hundred metre intervals

who lives next door to the church which has a modern statue of St Jacques.

Now begins a long climb to the hilltop village of Aubrac. Once again, the route is very exposed in places with little shelter. After a long, hard climb to the **Station de Ski** in 4km, you can rest at a bar/restaurant. **Aubrac**, 5km further on, is very small with expensive hotels and restaurants but no shops. (There is a *gîte d'étape* in the medieval Tour des Anglais (Tel.65.44.25.51) but it does not open until 5.00pm and shelter is at a premium in this high, exposed village.) An undulating ride of 18km now follows. It is possible to branch off left to St Chély d'Aubrac (shop and *gîte d'étape*) after a kilometre but this entails a very steep descent followed by the inevitable ascent out of the village, which is picturesque but not breathtaking. (If this route is taken, be sure to cross the bridge in the village. Failure to do so can result in a very stiff climb to regain the D987.)

If you stay on the D987, having reached **Saugues**, the road begins its 8km descent into **St Côme d'Olt**. The road steepens considerably and it is wise to stop at least once to allow the rims to cool.

St Côme d'Olt is an exquisite medieval town including a church with an alarmingly twisted spire. Its cobbled lanes and half-timbered houses are a joy. It has shops, hotels, restaurants, a bank and a gîte d'étape housed in a medieval tower (Tel. 65.44.07.24). Your bicycle can be stored in the basement next to the showers. Be prepared for everywhere except the gîte to be shut on Sundays. The Town Hall is the place to have your Pilgrim Passport stamped.

Day 5: St Côme d'Olt to Estaing (15km)

Leave **St Côme d'Olt** by the D987 which follows the Lot valley through pleasant, leafy suburbs for 5km to **Espalion**.

This is a very busy town where several important roads meet and cross the River Lot. Hotels, shops, restaurants, banks and a gîte d'étape can be found in Espalion. The parish church has an imposing facade but the interior is drab. The museum opposite has travelling exhibitions and the staff at the Town Hall are most helpful to pilgrims and will stamp your

Pilgrim Passport.

Cross the pilgrim bridge over the Lot and take the road immediately to the right of the hôtel de ville (D556). Care is needed here as it is easy to miss this road. After 3km take a lane to the left signed **Bessuéjouls**. Within 400m take a rough track to the left. (There is no need to go into Bessuéjouls village.) This will lead, in 200m, to the **Church of St Pierre**.

This is one of the most beautiful churches on the whole pilgrimage. The real gem of the building is a tiny chapel on the first floor of the tower. Here there are ninth-century tableaux and capitals with wonderful carvings. It

DAY 5

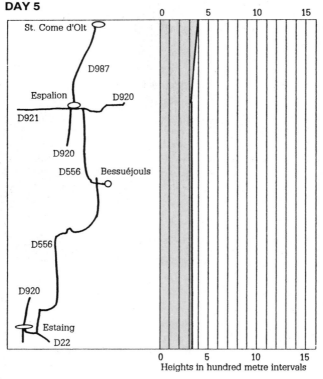

Heights in hundred metre intervals

Bessuéjouls - ninth-century chapel in the tower of St Pierre

is the time which can be well-spent here and in Estaing that makes the travelling day such a short one.

Retrace your steps to the D556 and turn left for Estaing. The road, which is a mixture of flat riding and short hills, crosses farmland devoted to market gardening rather than the ranching of the

27

Margeride. The scenery is fine with the river away to your right and on reaching **Verrières** in 6km, the road turns sharp right at a T-junction and runs high along the left bank of the beginning of the Lot gorge. After 2km, turn right at the junction with the D22 and cross the ancient bridge over the Lot to enter **Estaing**.

Estaing is another beautiful medieval village with a mighty chateau towering over it. Narrow streets twist and turn below it and a promenade makes a relaxing place to sit beside the Lot. You will find hotels, restaurants, banks and plenty of shops and a supermarket, but if you stay at the Hospitalité Saint Jacques (Tel. 65.44.19.00) none of this need worry you. You will be cared for and fed in peace and tranquillity and sent out refreshed in spirit and body the following day. Even your bicycle will be stored safely in their garage. The distinctive red stamp of the Hospitalité will be put into your Pilgrim Passport when you sign the visitors' book (the Livre d'Or). This is a day to savour, not to rush through, and no apologies are made because it is so short.

Day 6: Estaing to Conques (42km)

Leave **Estaing** by the medieval bridge over the Lot and, at the junction, take the D22, right, for Campuac. The road climbs for the next 8km with many hairpins before levelling out as it nears **Campuac**.

The church here is worth looking into. The exterior is simple but the interior is filled with beautiful modern stained glass and many modern sculptures and ecclesiastical pieces.

Leave the town by a small lane at the far right corner of the square (signed GR65). At the first main road, D904 (not signed), turn right and ignore any other signs which may be there. In 2km at **Vernhettes**, turn left for **Campagnac** on the D519. This road descends more and more steeply until it reaches the D42 on the outskirts of **Espeyrac** (restaurant and bar).

If you want to visit this small town, turn right and climb for 1km. If not, turn left and begin an 8km climb through the ancient village of **Senergues**.

After travelling 2km past this village, the D137 will be met. Go straight on it and within another 2km (the road is now the D42) you will begin a 6km descent into **Conques**. Ignore the 'no entry' sign (for cars) and drop directly down the main, cobbled street to the Cathedral.

Note: The route between Campuac and Espeyrac is very complex as there are many minor roads and the IGN map is definitely not accurate here. It is often very difficult to tell which roads are on the map and which are not. If you are at all unsure, it may be safer to take the D20, to the right just before entering Campuac, as far as Golinhac

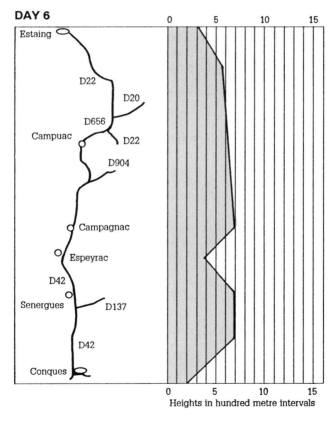

DAY 6

Heights in hundred metre intervals

Conques - Cathedral tympanum (The Last Judgement - detail)

and then turn left onto the D519 to Espeyrac.

Conques is rated one of the most beautiful sites in France. It is certainly a lovely medieval village but it is overrun with tourists. The best time to see it is in the late evening when the setting sun brings out the colours of the Cathedral tympanum or early morning when the cobbled streets are still empty and echoing. A visit to the Cathedral is a 'must'. The statue of St Foy in the museum is distinctive if a little over the top. Hotels, restaurants and shops abound (but no bank). Accommodation is available at the Communauté des Frères Prémontrés (tel. 65.69.85.12) or, surprisingly cheaply, at the Auberge St Jacques (Tel. 65.72.82.47) opposite the entrance to the Cathedral. (Bicycles stored in the bar at night.)

Day 7: Conques to Livinhac-le-Haut (30km)

Conques is a long, straggling village dropping by a winding cobbled street, the Rue Charlemagne, to the River Dourdou. Cross it, using the medieval bridge next to the Auberge du Pont Romain,

Conques - looking back from the climb to Noailhac

and climb the road which begins at the far side of it.

The next 6km are an unrelenting, steep climb. There are some excellent views looking back to Conques and there is considerable shade if the weather is hot, but you will be heartily sick of the hill by the time you reach its summit close to the junction with the D606. Turn left here but there is no need to go into **Noailhac** (*gîte*, café, restaurant) unless you have some special reason. Instead keep on

DAY 7

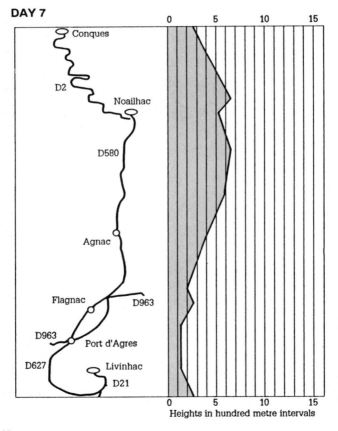

Heights in hundred metre intervals

Le Puy . Looking back from the road to Cordes (Day 1)
Saugues. The approach from Monistrol (Day 2)

the D580 to the right which quickly takes you to the chapel of St **Roch**.

This beautiful, isolated chapel with its evocative statue on the facade has a most attractive stained glass window inside and a picnic area opposite.

The road now climbs and plunges across hilly terrain with radio masts on the summits. After 8km, at **La Bessenoits**, ignore the road to the left into Decazeville (cycle shop) but keep to the D580 signed Agnac. Decazeville with its scars from opencast mining can clearly be seen to your left but stay above it, on a badly surfaced road, through the suburb of **Agnac**.

The road now sweeps down for 4km in a series of hairpins until it reaches the D963. Here turn right onto it with the River Lot close by on your left. In 3km, a diversion to the right and uphill takes you into the small, sleepy town of **Flagnac**.

This is the first place to find food and a bar since leaving Conques but be aware that everything, including the bar, shuts at lunch-time.

Continue through the town. The road swings left and drops to join the D963 again just before the **Port d'Agrès** (a hotel and bar are immediately on the left over the bridge). Cross the bridge, and take the first road on the left (in 200m), the D627. This keeps the River Lot on its left until it meets the D21 at **Basse-Ville**. Here turn left and follow the road as it sweeps below **Livinhac-le-Haut**. Take the first road to the left signed 'Centre Ville' and climb up to the village square.

This quiet village has shops, bars, restaurants near the campsite on its outskirts, a hotel and a gîte d'étape (the key can be obtained from the Bar de la Mairie in the main square). Bicycles have to be stored outside. The church clock alongside the gîte d'étape is now silenced after 9.00pm so that a good night's rest is assured.

Conques - The Rue Charlemagne looking towards the cathedral

Day 8: Livinhac to Marcilhac-sur-Célé (50km)

Retrace your previous day's route as far as **Basse-Ville**. The climb out of **Livinhac** west along the D2 is quite long and fairly steep but not as steep as the first kilometre suggests. After passing through **Montredon**, the road (the D2) continues to climb steadily as far as **St Félix** which is just off the road. (The church of St Radegonde with its primitive tympanum is worth a visit.)

The D2 now undulates with several lengthy climbs as far as the outskirts of **Figeac** where it becomes very busy as it descends to the River Célé. Cross the river and turn right, then immediately left, to enter the old part of the town. (Beware the one-way system.)

Figeac is a pleasant medieval town with many restored houses and all facilities including hotels, restaurants, banks, tourist office, shops, cycle shop and supermarkets, most of which close at lunch-time. It can be very busy. The church has a most interesting crypt with unusual decoration.

Leave Figeac by the D13 west keeping the river on your left. (The immediate exit is confusing as it turns away from the river bearing right for half a kilometre but it is well signed to Cahors.) In 6km, turn left off the D13 onto the D41, again keeping the river immediately to your left. You are now entering the Célé gorge which runs for 50km to join the Lot gorge, becoming ever more spectacular the further you enter it.

In 5km, pass through the farming village of **Boussac**, 2km later, the village of **Corn**, and another 7km further on, you will see the monastery of **Espagnac** (bar) nestling on the far side of a bridge over the Célé. If you have time, this is well worth a visit and it is possible to stay there. If, however, you are not tired of the almost flat road, continue along the D41 through **Brengues** with its tiny bar and **St Sulpice** (bar) where houses are built into the rock until you reach the small town of **Marcilhac-sur-Célé**.

Here there are hotels, a chambre d'hôte, bars, an excellent restaurant, shops and a tiny gîte d'étape (bicycles stored inside) built in the ruins of the abbey which is, itself, well worth a visit. The syndicat d'initiative, also in the abbey grounds, is extremely helpful to pilgrims.

DAY 8

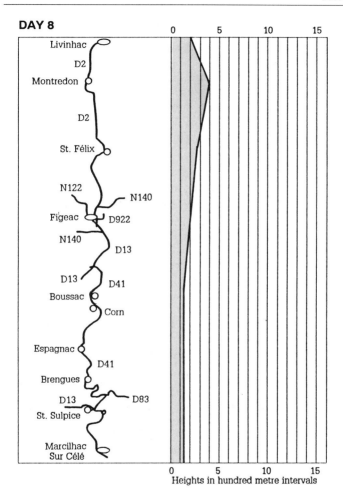

Heights in hundred metre intervals

Day 9: Marcilhac-sur-Célé to Cahors (60km)

Leave **Marcilhac** in a westerly direction by the D41. The road now enters the most spectacular part of the Célé gorge with high cliffs and a series of short road tunnels, through **Sauliac-sur-Célé** to reach **Cabrerets** (hotels, bars, shops) in 14km. (If time permits, a visit to the Grotte de Pech-Merle is recommended but it does entail a climb.)

A further 4km brings you to the T-junction with the D662 where the Célé runs into the River Lot. **Turn left onto the D662** and follow this busy road for 4km, keeping the River Lot to your right. At the sign for **St-Cirq-Lapopie**, turn right over the river bridge and climb very steeply into this most famous village. St-Cirq-Lapopie is a tiny medieval village perched above the Lot gorge with many craftsmen plying their trade. You may have to fight your way through throngs of tourists to see the place!

Hotels, restaurants and bars as well as a tourist office are easily found. A gîte at Tour de Faure is 2km away. The church is in a bad state of repair

Cahors - the street market

DAY 9

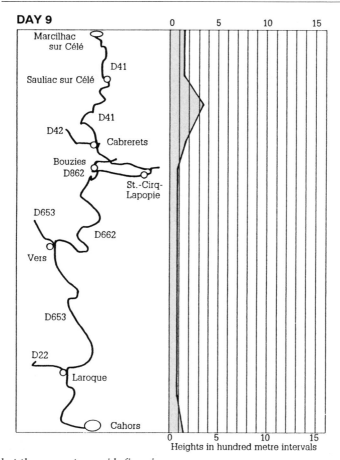

0   5   10   15

Marcilhac
sur Célé

D41

Sauliac sur Célé

D41

D42

Cabrerets

Bouziès
D862

St.-Cirq-
Lapopie

D653

D662

Vers

D653

D22

Laroque

Cahors

0   5   10   15
Heights in hundred metre intervals

but the ramparts provide fine views.

Do not retrace your steps but ride on along the D40 to **Bouziès**. This involves a short, sharp climb followed by a fascinating ride along a terrace, high on the side of the Lot gorge, before descending spectacularly to Bouziès (hotel/restaurant). Here, cross the bridge over the Lot and turn left onto the D662.

The Célé Gorge near Cabrerets

This busy and far less interesting road will lead you in 14km to **Vers** (bar) and, in another 8km, to **Laroque-des-Arcs** (restaurant and bar). After this, the outskirts of Cahors appear, the city being reached in another 6km. The final section of this ride is a steady climb to the highest point of **Cahors** before a descent along the main street into the centre. Expect to find very heavy traffic here.

Cahors is a large, bustling, commercial and market town with congested traffic, a convoluted one-way system and few hotels. Those near the railway station are expensive and those close to the centre are basic. The Hostellerie de Douelle (Tel. 05.65.35.25.93) is simple, cheap and clean and close to the town centre. Bicycles are stored in the hotel courtyard. The Office de Tourisme *offers excellent town plans free of charge. The Cathedral and the Pont Valentré are worth close examination.*

Day 10: Cahors to Moissac (66km)

Do not leave **Cahors** by the Pont Valentré but follow the main road through the town south and leave on the N20. After 3km, turn right onto the D7 as far as **Labastide-Marnhac**. In the village, turn left onto the D67 to ride across open moorland before meeting the D659 at a T-junction in 3km. Turn right onto this road and in just over a kilometre, the village of **L'hospitalet** (shop and restaurant) will be reached.

Turn right here onto the D54. This is a beautiful valley road passing through farmland and gently descending for 10km until it reaches a minor crossroads with the D7. Turn left here for **St-Laurent-Lolmie** and Lauzerte. This road, too, descends a wide river valley devoted to melon growing, passing through the hamlet of St Laurent (bar) in 7km. Another easy 8km from here the D953 is met and joined. Turn left, leaving **Lauzerte** standing proudly above the road on the right. There is no need to visit this town (bars, shops, restaurants, hotels and *gîtes d'étape* - key from Mairie or Tel. 63.94.64.05) unless there is some pressing need. Instead 2.5km further along the D953, **turn left onto the D58**.

This road runs parallel to the D953 (visible on the right) but is deserted while the former road is busy. After 7km, when the D957 is met, turn left onto it until the River Barguelonne is crossed. From this bridge, the road climbs steeply for 5km until the village of **Ste. Thiècle** (bar) is attained.

Now the road descends, steepening gradually until, after 3.5km

DAY 10

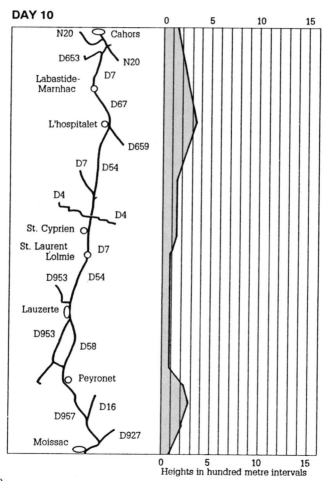

Heights in hundred metre intervals

the D16 joins it from the left (take care as vehicles joining from the left appear to have right of way) and after another 5km, turn right, at the outskirts of **Moissac**, onto the D927. After a further 1km, this will lead you into the centre of the town.

Moissac, sitting astride the River Tarn, is dominated by its Abbey of St Pierre whose tympanum and cloisters are breathtaking. It has many hotels, bars, restaurants, supermarket, banks and shops including a cycle repair shop and an excellent gîte d'étape (with secure cycle storage) at the municipal campsite which is to be found on the far side of the canal and river, immediately to the left approximately 1km from the town centre (Tel. 05.63.32.52.52).

Day 11: Moissac to Lectoure (58km)

Leave **Moissac** in a westerly direction on the N113. This drab exit to the town keeps the River Tarn to its left as it climbs out of Moissac until, after 4.5km, the D15 to the left is taken. (Take care. This is an awkward junction if traffic is heavy.) This leads to **St Nicholas de la Grave** (bar, shops) in 3.5km. Its church tower with strange hole through it can be seen from afar.

Continue on the D15, having dog-legged round the church, until the road crosses the *autoroute* and at the crossroads immediately afterwards, turn right onto the D12 which will take you to Auvillar. A more interesting route is to follow the D12 for 4km, then turn left and follow signs up into **St Michel**.

Once through the village, turn right for **Bardigues** (bar) on narrow and extremely steep roads. Ride through the village and turn left at the T-junction and immediately right, dropping rapidly to join the D953. Turn left here and ride into **St Antoine**. If you decide to ride into Auvillar, then leave it, west, by the D88 until you meet the D953, turning left onto it to reach St Antoine, the site of an ancient pilgrim hospital. (The last house in the village is still a *gîte d'étape* but there are no shops.)

The D953 is now followed as it undulates steeply across open countryside before climbing the long, steep hill into **Flamarens**. Once through this picturesque village, the road continues its switchback ride until another steep ascent reaches **Miradoux** (shop).

41

Take the D23 out of the village and gradually descend for 6km until the River Auroue is crossed. Continue on the D23 through the hamlet of **Castet-Arrou** and for the next 7km, climb and descend as the road crosses pleasant farmland before reaching the N21, 3km

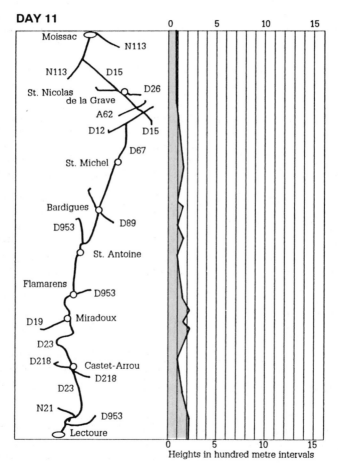

DAY 11

Heights in hundred metre intervals

from **Lectoure**. Turn left onto this road and make the last ascent of the day into the town centre.

Lectoure is built on a bluff of land overlooking the valley of the Gers. It has hotels, bars, restaurants, banks and shops as well as an excellent Office de Tourisme *and a modern if somewhat grubby* gîte d'étape *with indoor bike storage. The church of St Gervais & St Portais is well worth a visit and a stroll along the high promenade above the valley is highly recommended.*

Day 12: Lectoure to Condom (22km)

This is a short but, nevertheless, extremely tough stage with time, at the end of it, for exploring the fascinating country market town of Condom. Leave **Lectoure** in a westerly direction on the D7 descending for 2km in a sweeping arc with fine views below the town before crossing the River Gers. It is worth looking back at Lectoure at this point to see how well defended it is on its rocky promontory.

Now begins an arduous ride of 18km due west on the D7 with a series of hills, each approximately 1km up, the same down and about half a kilometre between each one. The countryside is pleasant if not spectacular with most of the agricultural land given over to growing sunflowers or arable crops. There is no town or village for about 15km and little in the way of shelter. If you want a drink on the way, make sure your water bottles are full before you leave Lectoure as there is no bar before you reach Caussens. The steepest hills are early in the journey but the general impression is of an endless succession of climbs until the hill-top village of **Caussens** (road-side bar and restaurant) is reached.

The final 6km into **Condom** is still hilly but the gradients are not as severe as those encountered earlier in the day until a final climb through narrow streets brings you into the centre of this ancient town.

The Gascon market town of Condom is built on a hill with the River Baise flowing along its western side. It has flourished as one of the chief centres of the Armagnac distribution industry and has a museum celebrating this fact. The main square with its towering flamboyant Gothic Cathedral

DAY 12

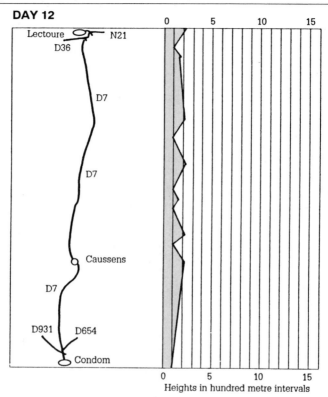

Heights in hundred metre intervals

of St Pierre is at the highest point with narrow, medieval streets, many of which are pedestrianised, radiating from it. It has hotels, bars, supermarket, banks, shops, a cycle shop and restaurants as well as a good Office de Tourisme *and an excellent* gîte d'étape *on the top floor of the Centre Salvandy, a college. The latter is quite difficult to find but worth the effort. From the Place St Pierre outside the Cathedral, take the Rue Bonamy which becomes the Rue Cadeot. At the top, turn right into the Rue Jean Joures. The* gîte *is on the right in 100m. The concierge, who lives in the inner courtyard of the college, does not open the* gîte *until 5.00pm but there is a shady courtyard with seats to rest if you arrive early.*

Day 13: Condom to Eauze (33km)

Leave **Condom** by crossing the river and taking the D15 signed for Montreal. The hilly nature of the terrain continues where it left off the previous day.

After 5km, take a left turn, well signed, to **Larressingle**. This is a detour of 3km and the route from the main road you have just left

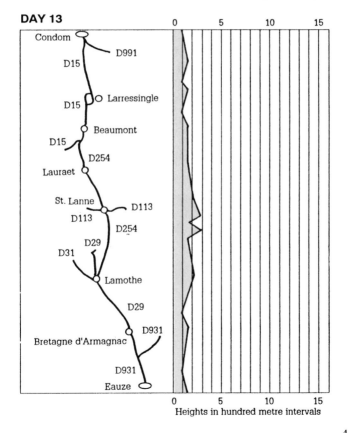

DAY 13

Condom
D991
D15
D15 — Larressingle
Beaumont
D15
D254
Lauraet
St. Lanne — D113
D113
D254
D29
D31
Lamothe
D29
Bretagne d'Armagnac — D931
D931
Eauze

Heights in hundred metre intervals

The fortified village of Larressingle - entrance

has to be retraced. Climb very steeply until this perfect, medieval fortified village is reached.

Only pedestrians and cyclists are allowed over the drawbridge to view this incredible gem of a village with its church, castle, bar, restaurant and souvenir shops.

Return to the D15 and continue to climb and descend at regular intervals for another 3km. At this point it appears from the signs that **Château Beaumont** is a bus shelter on the left! Just beyond it, take the D254 to the left, sign-posted Lauraët.

This deserted, narrow country road switch-backs between vines and fields of maize and after 3km reaches **Lauraët** which is no more than a large hamlet in a beautiful setting with stone benches for the weary to rest. Continue along the D254 for another 3km until the D113 is crossed next to the vineyard at St Lanne. There are yet more spectacular climbs and descents along the D254 until the D29 is reached at a T-junction close to **Lamothe**.

Turn left here (there is no need to enter the village). Instead follow the D29 for another 3.5km into **Bretagne-d'Armagnac** (bar and restaurant).

This is one of the villages producing the world famous Armagnac whose centres of distribution are Condom, Eauze and Aire-sur-L'Adour.

Continue along the D29 for another 2.5km and then turn right onto the D931 which leads directly into **Eauze** in another 4.5km.

Eauze is a small market town with hotels, restaurants, bars, banks, supermarket, cycle shop and shops. There is a basic gîte d'étape above the Office de Tourisme, close to the town centre, where the key is lodged. The Gothic fifteenth-century cathedral of St Luperc is worth a visit and there are several attractive half-timbered houses.

Day 14: Eauze to Aire-sur-L'Adour (45km)

Take the D931, south, out of **Eauze**, sign-posted Nogaro. This excellent quiet road has none of the harsh hills encountered in previous days and the surface is almost perfect for cycling.

In 9km, cross the railway at **Manciet** (hotels, bars, restaurant and shops). The main road now becomes the N124 and maintains its pristine condition. Although there are several hills, the gradients are far easier than previously encountered, and 7km further on, the market town of **Nogaro** is reached (hotels, bars, restaurants, supermarket and shops). (The church at the far end of the town is worth a visit.)

At this point, there are two alternative routes to Aire-sur-L'Adour. The N124 can be followed for the next 25km into the centre

DAY 14

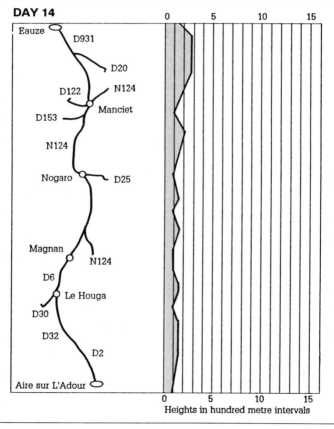

Heights in hundred metre intervals

St-Cirq-Lapopie in the Lot gorge

Left:
St Jean-Pied-de-Port.
View down the Rue
de la Citadelle
(Day 17)

Right:
Ibañeta.
Monument of Roland
(Day18)

of the town. It is not too hilly and has an excellent surface but it does not pass through any town or village of note until it reaches Barcelonne-du-Gers, an out-of-town retail area, 4km from Aire-sur-L'Adour.

The alternative, and more interesting route follows the N124 for 6km from Nogaro to the village of **Arbiade-le-Haut**. Here take the right-hand turn, the D6, for Le Houga, passing through the pleasant villages of **Magnan** and **Perchède** before arriving in **Le Houga** (hotel and bar) in 9km.

In the centre of the village, turn left onto the D32 which, after passing a very attractive lake with picnic facilities, in 4km becomes the D2 which, in a further 8km, takes you directly into the centre of **Aire-sur-L'Adour**.

At about the half-way point of this road, in the forest to your left, is a most welcoming chambre d'hôte *at Le Glindon (Tel. 62.08.97.61). The owners particularly welcome pilgrims and offer a discount.*

Aire-sur-L'Adour, which is entered over the main river bridge, is a bustling market town which rewards those who stay to explore it. It has hotels, bars, restaurants, several chambres d'hôte, a gîte d'étape *in the Centre de Loisir as well as shops, a cycle shop and a supermarket. The Cathedral is rather sombre but the church of Ste. Quitterie du Mas is fascinating. The keys (and a guided tour) are available from a few doors away. It is an experience which should not be missed.*

Day 15: Aire-sur-L'Adour to Sauvelade (72km)

WARNING - This stage has no flat section in it at all with the most severe climbs in the final 10km. Take food and drink with you as this is very scarce during much of the journey.

Leave **Aire-sur-L'Adour** by the steep hill which passes the church of St Quitterie, the N134. Once clear of the town, turn right onto the D2 for **Geaune** which will be reached in 13km. Here take the D111 which will bring you to **Pimbo** (bar) in another 12km. Take a left turn at Pimbo onto the D32 for **Arzacq-Arraziguet** (shops and bar/

café - may be closed at lunch-time). These small country towns have little to detain you and seem, at times, to be deserted.

Leave the wide town square of Arzacq on the D946, heading across country for Morlanne. This extremely hilly road is virtually deserted with few houses or farms in sight. In 14km, **Morlanne** will bring little relief. (The well-decorated exterior of the church is interesting but the entrance will probably be locked.) Continue on

DAY 15

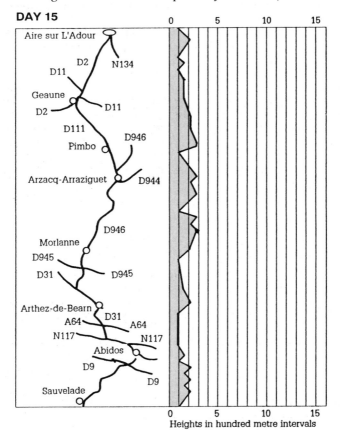

Heights in hundred metre intervals

the D946 for 8km, crossing the D945, until you reach a T-junction with the D31. Turn left and climb the very steep hill into **Arthez-de-Béarn**, 3km away. Here there are bars, a cycle shop and a small supermarket but no hotel. From Arthez, take the D31, south, crossing the *autoroute* in 5km and reaching the N117 in another kilometre. (A hotel is here, but in a very noisy position.)

Turn left onto the N117 for a kilometre to **Lacq**, then take the D33 crossing the bridge into **Abidos**. This is a busy, unpleasant stretch of road, lined with industry and railway sidings. Turn right in Abidos and climb the steep hill into **Lagor** centre (bar, hotel, last shops before Sauvelade which has none) which will be reached in 3km.

Turn left off the main street (there are no signposts on this section) where it begins to descend, into a road bordered with high walls, which drops steeply to the right. After the bridge, take the right fork and then turn left after the car breaker's yard. Climb steeply past a white house on the right. Soon after this, ignore the road to the left on the brow of the hill. Instead descend to a T-junction. Turn right, climbing and dropping steeply until a minor crossroads is reached at a small steep summit with a slight dog-leg left. Continue straight over this and at the bottom of the next hill, Sauvelade will appear on your left (modern *gîte d'étape*, **no shops**).

Day 16: Sauvelade to St Palais (43km)

On leaving **Sauvelade** (most interesting Benedictine and, later, Cistercian abbey and rather austere church of St Jacques) bear left onto the D110 and, after 5km, follow the signs to the right on this valley road into the village of **Vielleségure** (shops). Ride through the centre and descend steeply to the D111.

Here turn right onto this wide, well-surfaced road, heading for **Navarrenx** which you will reach after a series of stiff climbs in 9km.

Navarrenx is an interesting, walled, medieval bastide town with hotels, bars, shops, tourist office which will stamp your Pilgrim Passport and provide an excellent plan of the town and a supermarket. On market days, the centre of the town can become very congested.

Cross the River Gave d'Oloron and turn immediately right for **Castelnau-Cambiong**, which is reached in 1km, then take the D115 for Nabas. The road again climbs and falls rapidly through wooded scenery for 11km before dropping to cross the River Saison and the railway to enter **Nabas** (bar which may be closed).

The D115 continues to cross more undulating country (you are now in the foothills of the Pyrenees) until, in 3km, it reaches **Aroue**.

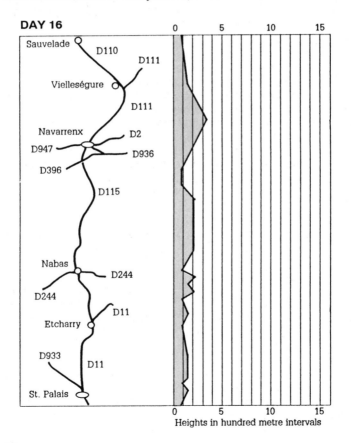

DAY 16

Heights in hundred metre intervals

Aroue is a prosperous little village with an interesting church dedicated to St Etienne in which can be found a statue of St Jacques Matamoros (the Moor-slayer), rarely seen in France but very common in Spain.

Turn right here onto the D11, signed St Palais. (In 1km, on the right, a small garage sells drinks etc. and is very sympathetic to pilgrims, offering its shady trees as a picnic spot. It also holds the key for the local *gîte d'étape*.) Another 10km along the constantly undulating D11, having passed through the villages of **Etcharry, Domezain Berraute and Benasque-Lapiste**, the road enters **St Palais**. (Ignore the road which drops steeply to the right as you enter the town.)

St Palais has hotels, bars, restaurants, shops, a cycle shop, tourist office and supermarket. Pilgrims can also be accommodated at the very welcoming Communauté Franciscaine, 1, Ave. de Gibraltar (Tel. 59.65.71.37), on the outskirts of the town, heading towards St Jean-Pied-de-Port. This is a very busy market town with a strong Spanish influence.

Day 17: St Palais to St Jean-Pied-de-Port (32km)

You may be tempted to leave **St Palais** by way of the D302 to see the Stele de Gibraltar where the paths from Le Puy, Vezelay and Paris meet but, if the gradient is too daunting, take the D933 out of the town and whisk along its smooth, level surface, keeping the River Bidouze alongside.

After 10km of enjoyable riding, you can take a right-hand turn to **Harambels** to see its eleventh-century chapel but you must return to the D933 by the same route. The same goes for visiting **Ostabat** (shops, bar and *gîte d'étape*) in another 3km. There used to be two roads into this hill-top village but recent roadworks seem to have closed the first and it may be necessary to take the second road and ride back into the village, returning by the same road. It adds no more than 2km onto the day's journey.

Having passed the junction with the D918 at **Larcevaux** (hotels, bars, restaurants and shops to the left of the main road) the road begins to climb and descend as it approaches the Pyrenees proper but there is nothing too steep anywhere on this stage.

Lacarre has a hotel, bar and restaurant but nothing else to detain you until, in 12km, you reach **St Jean-le-Vieux** (hotels, restaurants, shops). In 1.5km after leaving the village, turn left off the D933 onto an unsigned country lane to **La Magdeleine.** Having passed through the village, climb very steeply to the Citadel overlooking **St Jean-Pied-de-Port** and bear right to enter the town through the pilgrim gate, the Porte Saint-Jacques. This road is cobbled and it is advisable

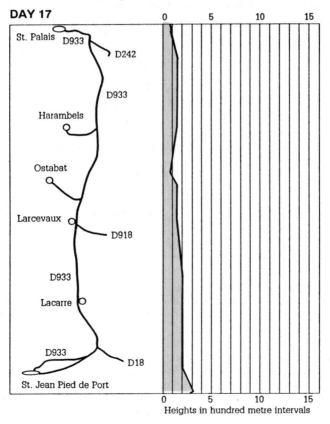

DAY 17

Heights in hundred metre intervals

to dismount before descending the steep Rue de la Citadelle.

St Jean-Pied-de-Port is a busy tourist town with shops including a cycle repair shop, supermarket, tourist office, hotels, restaurants and bars. If possible, have your passport stamped by Madame Debril who lives half-way down the Rue de la Citadelle on the right, but go at a reasonable hour. If not, the Pilgrim Office in the Rue de la Citadelle will oblige. There are two gîtes d'étape in the town, one close to the Pilgrim Office and a cramped private one at 9, Rue d'Uhart. The citadel, built in 1688, is worth visiting for its views of the Pyrenees and the following day's route. The fourteenth-century Gothic church of St Jean is also interesting.

Day 18: St Jean-Pied-de-Port to Roncesvalles (34km)

This is the longest climb of the pilgrimage so far but do not be put off by horror stories. Much of the early part of the route is easy and there is plenty of shade if it is hot. There are lots of resting points and an ample supply of water.

Leave **St Jean-Pied-de-Port** by the D933, clearly signed to Pamplona, Roncesvalles, and Spain. This begins as a pleasant ride through rolling wooded hills with the river to your right.

After 8km, the village of **Arneguy** (bar and shops) is passed through and shortly afterwards a sign at the redundant customs post informs you that you have now entered Spain. (Remember to extend a greeting to oncoming cyclists now of *Hola* rather than *Bonjour!*)

From here, the road begins to climb more steeply but never becomes truly daunting. The surface is good and there is little heavy traffic apart from the odd timber truck. Another 3km further will see you in **Valcarlos**. (Here there are hotels, bars, restaurants and shops. There is also a bank in what looks like a private house where you can change francs into pesetas.)

It is from here that the climb really begins. The gradients are constant for the next 17km with no villages. On reaching **Casa Guardiano** 3km before the summit, the gradient steepens and this last stretch is an unrelenting drag with the chapel at the top of the

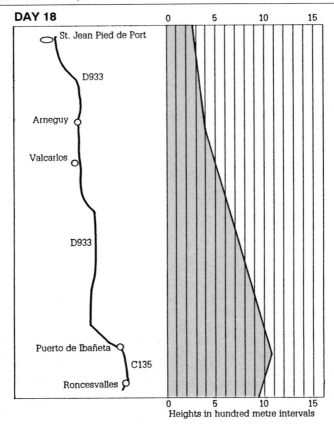

DAY 18

Heights in hundred metre intervals

Ibañeta Pass, your goal, visible in front of you.

The top of the pass is worth visiting, if only to recuperate for a few minutes. (The chapel is often closed but the mound of crosses is visible to the right of it, as is the monument to Roland. The views, if it is a clear day, are superb.)

The short descent to **Roncesvalles** is no more than 3km long.

Accommodation can be found in the refugio at the monastery or at one of the two hotels which also serve meals. (You must book a table in advance.)

56

*There are no food shops. The **refugio** does not open until 4.00pm but it is wise to arrive early and queue if you want a bed for the night as large numbers of pilgrims arrive by bus from Pamplona and all expect to find accommodation here.*

Day 19: Roncesvalles to Pamplona (45km)

Take the C135 from **Roncesvalles** towards Pamplona. This is a good, generally well-surfaced road which descends gently for 2km to the Basque village of **Burguete** (*hostales*, bars, restaurant and bank, none of which may open until 10.30am).

The road continues its gentle descent for another 2.5km at which point it swings sharply right 1km before the ancient Basque village of **Espinal** (bar, shops and restaurant) whose houses are decorated with coats of arms. Now begins a steady 12km ascent with a series of hairpin bends until it reaches the **Alto de Erro.** (The views from here are very good.) Ignore the C127 to the left but continue on the C135 as it begins a sharp winding descent for 10km until it reaches

Larrasoaña - Medieval pilgrim bridge

Zubiri (refuge, bar, restaurant, shop and bank). This grey little town has little to detain you so continue down the valley, keeping the river to your left.

In 5km, pause at the small town of **Larrasoaña** (refuge and bar). (The mayor is very supportive to pilgrims and will be keen to stamp your Pilgrim Passport and show you his collection of *camino*

DAY 19

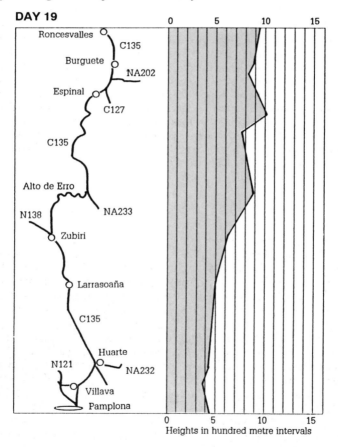

Heights in hundred metre intervals

memorabilia. The restored medieval bridge is worth a look.)

The gradient is now gentle, downhill, as the valley widens and in 10km, the town of **Huarte** appears. Turn right at the interchange with the new road system, heading for **Villava** (all facilities) and after 2km, turn left at traffic lights in the town centre. The very busy town you enter now is only a suburb of **Pamplona** so ride straight through it and follow signs until you reach the city centre.

Pamplona is difficult to negotiate even with a street map (available from the tourist office - if you can find it). There are many one-way streets and a number of intersecting medieval streets. All facilities are available including a refuge which refuses bikes. Hotel accommodation is bookable through the tourist office but can be expensive (disproportionately so during the San Fermin Festival). The Hotel Bearán (Tel. 22.34.28) in the Calle San Nicolas is reasonable and has secure bicycle storage and a lift. The best way to see the city is on foot. Restaurants and bars are plentiful and can be very good value. The Cathedral, especially the cloisters, should be visited - they will put a stamp (sello) in your Pilgrim Passport. There are several cycle repair shops.

Day 20: Pamplona to Estella (45km)

The route out of **Pamplona** is very difficult to find. There are no direction signs of use in the centre and it is not until you come across the correct exit that you will find the N111 (Puenta La Reina) signed on the outskirts of the city. The town plan available from the tourist office should help but you may have to ask for directions as you go along. Once the N111 has been attained and the *autovia* (A15) crossed, the route is obvious.

Leave **Cizur Mayor** on your right (no need to visit) and cycle towards the line of wind turbines you can see stretched out on a hilltop to your left and in front of you. The N111 here is wide and has a good cycle lane. Traffic is fast but not heavy and the surface is good. The road climbs steadily until the **Alto de Perdón** is reached in 14km.

About ¹/₂km after the top, turn left onto a country road heading for **Uterga** (bar which may be closed) which you will reach in 3km.

Another couple of kilometres further on, the village of **Muruzábal** will be reached. Here take a good track (not tarmac) to the left signed for Eunate. This sweeps through farmland until it reaches the main road opposite **Eunate** church (should not be missed). Alternatively, take the tarmac road out of Muruzábal until it reaches the main road and turn left until **Eunate** is reached. Having visited the church, turn left onto the road which joins the N111 1km short of Puenta la

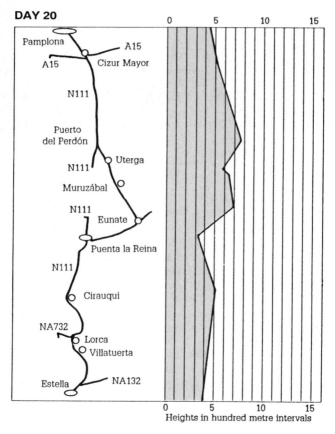

DAY 20

Heights in hundred metre intervals

Puenta la Reina - The Pilgrim Bridge

Reina at the point where the Pyrenean routes to Santiago all meet (marked with a modern statue).

Puenta la Reina (refuge, hotels, restaurants, bars and shops) is an interesting medieval town with its famous bridge over the River Arga. Its church of Santiago is worth a visit. Leave over the bridge, turning right, back onto the N111 signed for Estella. The road undulates a great deal but the surface is good. Most of the small hill-top towns and villages on this stretch - **Cirauqui** (bars), **Lorca** (bar), **Villatuerta** (bars) -are just off the main road and need not be visited unless there is some necessity.

In 19km, the road dips as it enters the town of **Estella**. Turn right off the main road into the town and climb up to its centre (refuge, hotels, restaurants, bars and shops and cycle repairs).

Although much of this town is very ancient, it is not particularly attractive. It has a large main square with a busy market. The Hostal San Andrés is adequate accommodation. The Palace of the Kings of Navarre, by the town hall (sello), is worth a visit.

61

Viana - Calle Mayor

Day 21: Estella to Viana (44km)

Leave **Estella** by the N111 and climb steadily through minor
industrial buildings out of the town until, after 3km, the monastery
of **Irache** (hotel, refuge) is seen on the left.

*This is worth visiting, although there is extensive restoration work in
progress, if only because alongside it is the famous wine fountain available*

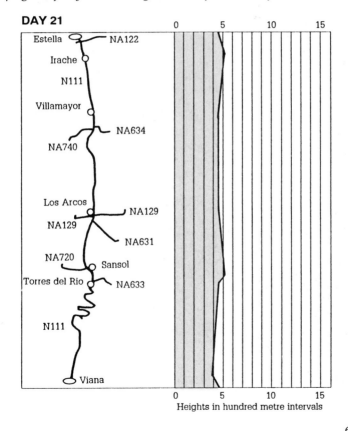

DAY 21

Heights in hundred metre intervals

free of charge to pilgrims - but be warned, it is potent stuff and you have a long hard ride still to come!

The road now climbs and drops over a none-too-inspiring countryside of scrub and wasteland, avoiding any place of interest for another 18km until a well-signed road to the right leaves the N111 and leads to **Los Arcos**, now by-passed by the main road with its shady town square (hotel, refuge, bar, restaurant and bank). (The flamboyant Gothic church of Santa María has an interesting cloister and choir stalls and several houses on the main street boast coats of arms.)

There is little here to detain you, however, so continue straight through the town and the N111 will be regained very shortly. This shadeless road now continues for another 7km until **Sansol** (shop) is reached. Leave the main road to visit the town. (It has a fine church dedicated to San Zoilo with interesting frescoes.) Regain the main road as it sweeps down past the most attractive village of **Torres del Río** (bar). Once again, leave the N111 to explore the village. (Its Romanesque twelfth-century church looks superb but it may be locked.) Return to the N111 before climbing steeply via a series of hairpins over wild open moorland with little shade or shelter. On reaching the summit, an exhilarating descent leads, 16km later, to a turn to the right into **Viana**. The road climbs steeply in a wide sweep round the town before attaining the central square which one comes upon almost by surprise.

Viana has a large, well-equipped refuge which welcomes cyclists and has secure storage for bikes. Most of the hotels, bars, restaurants and shops can be found on the Calle Mayor. The fifteenth-century church of Santa María, outside which Cesar Borgia is buried, is very fine. Many houses along the main street, the Calle Mayor, are decorated with armorial bearings. At one end of the main street is a primitive bull-ring where aspiring youths practise a non-lethal version of bull-fighting. There is an excellent view across the plain to Logroño from the ruined church and park of San Pedro alongside the refuge.

Left:
Léon Cathedral
(Day 28)

Below:
Frómista.
Church of St Martin
(Day26)

Day 22: Viana to Nájera (40km)

The descent from **Viana** to the main N111 is very fine with good views over Logroño and of the route to come. The road is wide with an excellent cycle lane and soon becomes the Logroño by-pass. If you wish to visit **Logroño**, turn right off the by-pass into the city centre.

Logroño contains refuge, hotels, shops including cycle repairs, banks,

DAY 22

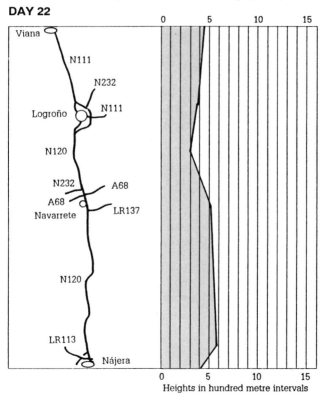

Heights in hundred metre intervals

bars and restaurant as well as the fine Cathedral of Santa María Redonda. The churches of San Bartolomé, Santa María de Palacio and the famous Santiago with its fine statue of Santiago Matamoros can also be visited.

You will need to return to the by-pass to leave the city. If you wish to avoid the city, continue along the by-pass following signs for N120 (Burgos).

As you follow these signs, you may be shocked to find you are now on a motorway. Cyclists are allowed on this - just stick to the hard shoulder. Stay on the motorway for 8km until the N120 (Burgos) is signed on a slip road. Follow this and it will quickly lead you to the turning, to the left, into **Navarrete**. (Do NOT turn onto the A68 as you are NOT allowed on this motorway with a bicycle.)

Navarrete has a fine sixteenth-century church with an incredible Baroque reredos which should not be missed, a fonda*, refuge, shops, restaurants, bank and bars. This is the last place of any significance before Nájera so it would be wise to purchase food and drinks here before continuing.*

The main street of Navarrete quickly leads back onto the N120 which is now slavishly followed to Nájera. It leads across hilly, open country with little remarkable or picturesque scenery before coming to the industrial outskirts of **Nájera**. Turn left here and descend through narrow streets until the bridge over the River Nájerilla is reached.

Nájera is an interesting old town backed by red sandstone cliffs. It has a refuge, hotel, hostel, fonda *(Fonda El Moro, Calle de los Martires 21, with secure cycle storage), shops including cycle repairs, banks, restaurants and bars. The Franciscan Monastery of Santa María la Real should not be missed, nor should the churches of San Miguel and Santa Cruz. The municipal swimming pool may give free access on production of a Pilgrim Passport. There is a pleasant, shady park alongside the river, close to the swimming pool.*

Nájera - Monastery of Santa María la Real

Day 23: Nájera to Santo Domingo de la Calzada (40km)

It is possible to ride the straight, boring N120 to Santo Domingo de la Calzada and reach the town in under two hours, but a longer and more hilly diversion is far more pleasant and includes a visit to two fascinating monuments.

To leave **Nájera,** cross back over the bridge and take the first

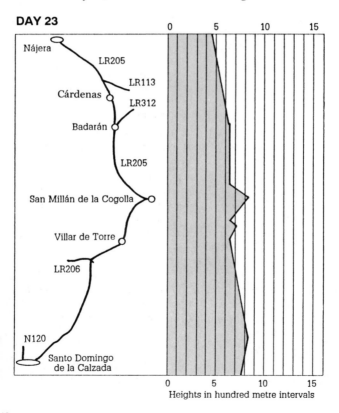

DAY 23

Nájera
LR205
LR113
Cárdenas
LR312
Badarán
LR205
San Millán de la Cogolla
Villar de Torre
LR206
N120
Santo Domingo
de la Calzada

Heights in hundred metre intervals

turning to the right, signed as the monasteries route. This is the LR113. It does not look very promising in the first couple of kilometres as the surface is poor and it leaves Nájera by way of small, dilapidated industrial units but soon these are left behind and the road follows close to the river between small market gardens.

After 6km, take a road to the right (LR205) to **Cárdenas**. Soon after this village, the road, which has been level, begins to climb and remains hilly for the rest of the day. Climb up to **Badarán** (shop and bar) in 4km. During the next 6km, the views across the rolling countryside are extensive with arrow-straight roads ignoring sharp ascents and descents. On reaching the LR206, turn left into **Berceo** (shop and bars). The monasteries of **San Millán de la Cogolla** are now clearly signed.

If you are only visiting the lower monastery, **Yuso** (bar), ride through the village of San Millán (bar) and ignore the uphill road to the monasteries. If you visit **Suso** (a very steep long climb), then take the uphill road to the right just beyond Berceo.

The monasteries are well worth a visit and the monks will guard your bikes and bags but be warned that the conducted tour round Yuso is long and only in Spanish.

Retrace your steps through San Millán village and Berceo but keep on the LR206 until the first crossroads. Here turn left for Santo Domingo de la Calzada which will be reached in another 14km. This road can be very exposed in extreme weather. **Villar de Torre** and **Cirueña** are little more than hamlets, in between which there are several long hills with little shade. The final 4km into **Santo Domingo de la Calzada** is a long descent onto the plain.

Santo Domingo (hotels, hostales, refuge, restaurants, banks, supermarket, shops, cycle repairs and bars) also boasts the Hospederia Santa Teresita (Tel.34.07.00), a convent run like a hotel. The Cathedral with its hen-coop and the old part of the town should not be missed.

Day 24: Santo Domingo de la Calzada to Burgos (66km)

The whole of this journey is spent on the N120. The road is wide and well surfaced with a cycle track throughout its length and, if you are fortunate enough to travel on a Sunday, devoid of traffic!

The first 6km are almost level until **Grañón** (bar and shops) is seen to the left of the road. The road now climbs steadily until **Castildelgado** (hotel, bar and *fonda*) is reached in another 6km. For the next 9km, the scenery is pleasant with woods appearing before a descent brings you to **Belorado** (refuge, *hostal*, bars, restaurants and shops). The outskirts of the town suffer from modern industrial blight but once the River Tirón is crossed, the woods appear along with steep hills until, in 12km, the road descends into **Villafranca Montes de Oca** (refuge and bar). This mountain village is not very appealing unless you are too shattered to attempt to climb the huge hill out of it.

The climb to the summit of the **Puerto de la Pedraja** is only short (about 2km) but, therefore, steep with little shade. A kilometre beyond the summit, the chapel of **Valdefuentes** appears on the right with an excellent, shady picnic stop opposite with tables and seats made out of old kilometre stones.

About 11km beyond this point, a road to the right quickly leads you into **St Juan de Ortega** (refuge and pilgrim church). Retrace your steps to the N120 and sweep downhill all the way into **Burgos**. This is probably the longest downhill stretch since leaving Le Puy. Follow the signs into the centre of Burgos. Do not deviate and the route is simple. Ignore all motorway signs.

Burgos is a beautiful city with wide tree-lined streets, a fascinating old quarter and a series of canals and rivers. It has a refuge, hotels, hostales, fondas and tourist office as well as a full range of shops including cycle repairs, supermarkets, bars, restaurants and banks. The Hostal San Juan (Tel. 20.51.34) offers a pilgrim discount and secure cycle storage. One of the most effective ways to view the main sights of Burgos is from the 'Little Train' which offers a one hour journey at very little cost. The Cathedral is breathtaking and should not be missed.

DAY 24

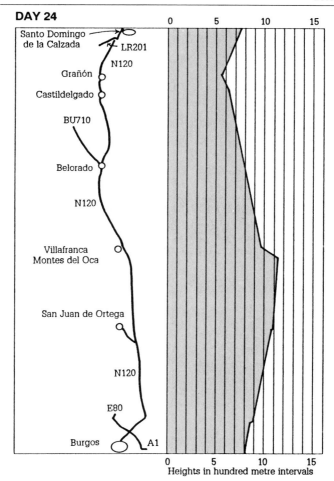

Heights in hundred metre intervals

Day 25: Burgos to Castrojeríz (48km)

This is the first of four days crossing the Meseta where the weather can be expected to be extreme. Ample food and drink should be taken and it should be remembered that the water supply is often curtailed between 8.00am and 8.00pm in summer.

The N120 out of **Burgos** is well signed and should prove no problem. There is even a special cycle track. On the immediate

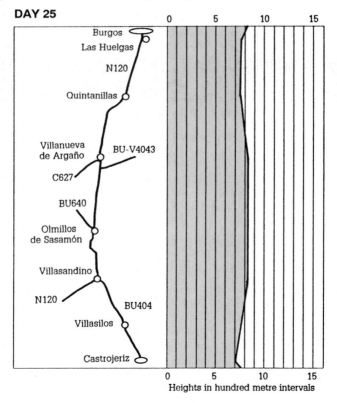

Heights in hundred metre intervals

Las Huelgas - Monastery cloisters

outskirts of the city, the Monastery of **Las Huelgas** (bars), which should not be missed although it does not open until 10.30am, is to be found to the left of the N120, clearly signed.

Return to the N120 and in 8km, the small town of **Tardajos** (refuge, *fonda*, restaurant, bar and shops) will be reached. This is the last real fuelling stop before Castrojeríz. Along this road, at regular intervals, picnic spots under the trees have been constructed and are most welcome.

In 10km, the road crosses the Rio Hormazuela at **Villanueva de Argaño**. From here, the road runs alongside a high escarpment to the right, a hunting ground for eagles and vultures which wheel high above on the thermals. The ancient town of **Olmillos de Sasamón** appears to the left of the road in 5km and in another 6km, just before **Villasandino**, the BU404 leaves the main road. Turn left onto this and in 50m there is a shady picnic spot on the right.

The road now heads out across the Meseta, passing close to abandoned villages with their brown, adobe walls blending with the bare soil. The road becomes lined with trees which can offer some shelter from summer sun and gradually climbs after the village of **Villasilos** is passed until a swift descent brings **Castrojeríz** into sight. To enter the small town, turn left off the road and follow the Calle Cordon into its centre.

The refuge wardens at Castrojeríz refuse cyclists and the post office does not carry stamps for outside Spain. There is, however, a welcome at the Hostal el Mesón (Tel. 37.74.00) where rooms are air-conditioned, although the food is rather ordinary. The three churches are worth a visit.

Day 26: Castrojeríz to Carrión de los Condes (46km)

Leave **Castrojeríz**, north, on the BU400. After 4km, turn left at **Castrillo de Matajudios**, a village of brown, adobe houses, onto the BU403 signed to Frómista. This road crosses a series of low ridges which means a series of short climbs and descents but once the Rio Pisuerga is crossed, the road, now the P432, becomes almost level. Both sides of this road are covered in masses of wild flowers which add colour to what would otherwise be a drab landscape of uncultivated fields.

A further 9km along this road, the village of **Boadilla del Camino** (bar and refuge) is reached. This fascinating place has a beautiful church with an exquisite font and an ancient pillory. It is quite common in this area to find local people walking along the roads rather than using any form of transport.

After a further 3km turn right onto the P431 which brings you into **Frómista** (refuge, hotel, *hostal, fonda,* restaurant, bars and shops).

The chief feature of this little town is the church of San Martín, said to be one of the most perfect Romanesque churches ever built. Its golden stone is carved into hundreds of creatures decorating the gables of the church.

From Frómista, follow the P980, reaching **Población** (refuge, shop and bars) in 3km. Picnic places still abound along this flat stretch of road with few bends. **Revenga de Campos**, a further 4km along the road, has nothing to distract the cyclist, nor has **Villarmentaro**, 2km further. The town of **Villalcazar de Sirga** (refuge, restaurant, bar and shop), however, does deserve a stop to see the church of Santa María la Blanca with its chapel of Santiago and fine entrance.

After another 7km, the town of **Carrión de los Condes** is reached. Follow the road straight into the town centre, which is not obvious.

Carrión de los Condes is a medieval town with hotels, refuge, restaurants, supermarket, shops including cycle repairs and bars. The Church of Santiago and the Monastery of San Zoilo are very fine. It also has the excellent Convento de Santa Clara for accommodation.

DAY 26

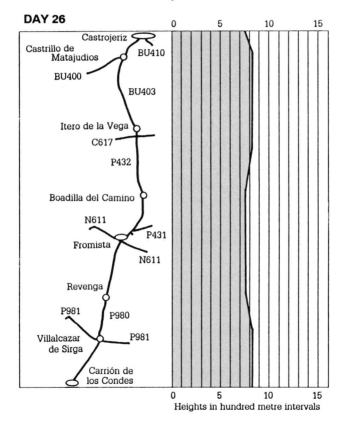

Heights in hundred metre intervals

Day 27: Carrión de los Condes to Sahagún (41km)

The exit from **Carrión de los Condes** is not easy to find. Head initially north (do NOT follow signs for León) until the N120 is met and then turn left in a westerly direction onto it, signed Sahagún.

The road, which seems to stretch in a straight line for miles, is level and wide with a good cycle track and picnic places at regular

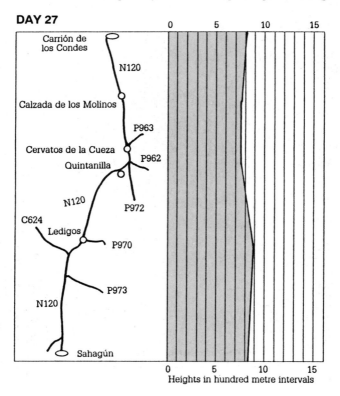

DAY 27

Carrión de los Condes
N120
Calzada de los Molinos
P963
Cervatos de la Cueza
P962
Quintanilla
N120
P972
C624
Ledigos
P970
P973
N120
Sahagún

Heights in hundred metre intervals

Sahagún - Modern statue of Santiago

intervals.

After 14km, the road skirts the village of **Cervatos de la Cueza** (bar and shop) before swinging sharply to the right. Do NOT continue on the P972 but keep to the N120. In less than 1km a sign to the left indicates the remains of a Roman villa at **Quintanilla de la Cueza**. A kilometre of rough country road reaches a large building on the right and this houses the restored remains of a Roman villa with extensive mosaic floors. (It is beautifully set out with excellent viewing and photographic points.) Having enjoyed this quite unique experience, return along the country road to rejoin the N120.

From here to Sahagún, the road is less level although the inclines are very gentle. There is a little more vegetation than one might expect but sources of food and drink are very scarce. **Calzadilla de la Cueza** (*hostal*, refuge and bar) and **Ledigos** (refuge, shop and bar) stand alongside the road as does **Terradillos de los Templarios** (*fonda*, bar and shop) but it may be difficult to purchase supplies at any of these villages where the amenities often appear to be shut.

In 11km from Terradillos de los Templarios, the road leads through the usual mixture of out-of-town light industry into **Sahagún**. The N120 by-passes the town to the right but the road is clearly signed and, if followed, will lead directly into the town centre.

Sahagún has a refuge, hotels, hostales, shops, cycle repairs, supermarket, banks and bars. If you are intending to stay at the refuge which welcomes cyclists and offers secure storage, head for the church of the Trinity on the right soon after entering the town. The lower portion is the tourist office and exhibition hall and the upper section houses the refuge. Sahagún has an interesting old quarter near its centre with a number of churches and monasteries which should be visited.

Day 28: Sahagún to León (67km)

Unless you have a real desire to follow the *camino* closely, the sensible route by bicycle from Sahagún to León is slightly longer than the walkers' route but is smooth, quick and simple.

León - Bronze statues outside Cathedral

Leave **Sahagún** by crossing the Rio Cea at traffic lights and following the road until it joins the N120 (turn left). This wide, quiet stretch of road winds gently through several unremarkable villages

DAY 28

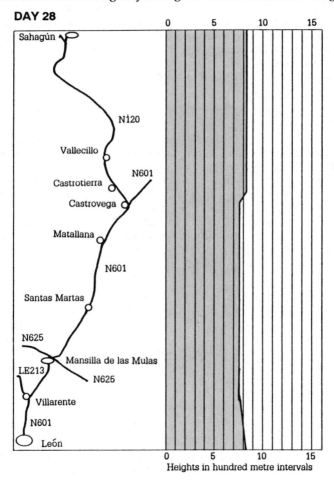

Heights in hundred metre intervals

with no facilities whatsoever until, after 28km, a bar appears to be the only marker of the **T-junction with the N601**.

Turn right here onto a much busier road with bars and *hostales*, usually accompanying petrol stations, at regular intervals. The cycle track is very wide and well surfaced. For the next 17km, the walkers' routes via El Burgo Ranero join the road from the right but cyclists should ignore them all and having crossed the railway line at **Valdearcos**, another 4km of easy riding will see you in the pleasant town of **Mansilla de las Mulas**.

The town has a refuge, hotel, restaurants, bars and shops and cycle repairs, a helpful tourist office, Roman walls and thirteenth-century church and chapel.

Cross the Rio Esla as you leave Mansilla de las Mulas and continue along the N601, crossing a second river, the Rio Porma, at **Villarente** (hostel and bar).

For the next 12km into León, the road becomes extremely busy and the cycle track disappears. Both sides of the road are lined with industrial buildings and the sooner you can pass through this cheerless landscape, the better. The road climbs steadily as it nears León but the gradient is easy. Do not turn off this main road but cycle directly into the centre of **León**. The traffic will be no busier than you have already encountered and the one-way system draws you inevitably into the heart of this interesting city.

León (refuge, hotels, hostales, fondas, restaurants, bars, banks, supermarkets and shops including cycle repairs) is full of fascinating places to visit. The tourist office, opposite the Cathedral, will provide details of places to see, accommodation and a town plan. The Hostal Reina (Tel. 20.52.00) has secure cycle storage and is very central. The Cathedral, Gaudi building, San Marcos and Pantheon with its remarkable wall paintings are essential viewing.

Day 29: León to Astorga (44km)

To leave **León**, cross in front of San Marcos Parador, ride over the bridge and once more join the N120, following signs for Astorga. In less than 1km the ring road will appear on your left. Do not turn left

León - Courtyard of the Palacio de los Guzmanes

onto it but continue heading west until in 2km you will reach the suburb of **Virgen del Camino** (*hostales*, bars, restaurant and shops). (The modern church has unusual bronze statuary both inside and out, including Santiago pointing towards your goal, and is very welcoming.)

Continue along the N120, avoiding the motorway (A66). The road, for the first time in three days, becomes hilly, until **Villadangos del Páramo** (*fondas*, refuge, bars, restaurant and shops) is reached. 5km beyond here, the road skirts the village of **San Martín del Camino** (bars) before leading, in another 6km, to a road to the right signed **Hospital d'Orbigo** (refuges, *hostales, fondas*, restaurants, bars and shops). This is well worth visiting with an interesting church. The parish house, which is run as a refuge, will provide you with a stamp for your Pilgrim Passport and offer you refreshment and a warm welcome even if you are not staying there. Sadly, walkers still take precedence.

The road surface hereabouts is very poor and it is advised you retrace your steps to the N120 and turn right onto it. Do not accept 'helpful' suggestions to take a short-cut and ride along rough tracks to Astorga. The next 15km into Astorga are across hilly terrain with little protection from sun or wind. There is a bar 3km short of Astorga in the village of **San Justo de la Vega**.

Astorga *is a pleasant town of Roman origins with massive walls still standing. In summer months, accommodation can be scarce with the refuge, hotels,* **hostales** *and* **fondas** *full early in the day. Residencia Santa María de los Angeles (Tel. 61.58.00) offers pilgrim accommodation and secure bike storage but is unmarked (take street opposite front of Cathedral*

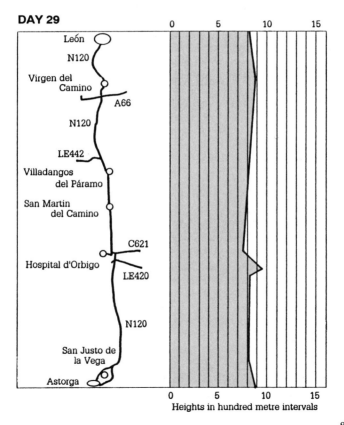

DAY 29

Heights in hundred metre intervals

and turn left into first lane, San Javier, 17). Residencia is through doorway on right. There are plenty of cheap restaurants and bars. The Cathedral and its museum are excellent and should not be missed, nor should Gaudi's Bishop's Palace which is as splendid inside as it is out. There are many shops, banks, supermarkets and a cycle repair shop.

Day 30: Astorga to Molinaseca (47km)

This stretch of the route as far as the summit at Cruz de Ferro is known as the Maragatería with unusual Maragatos villages which are worth spending some time in.

Leave **Astorga** by the Calle San Pedro. Cross the NV1 at traffic lights and follow the minor road opposite, signed for Santa Columba de Somoza. This road has a good surface but is being 'improved' by creating what appears to be a dual carriageway. The first place of interest is **Castrillo de los Polvazares** (shop and restaurants) which is reached in 4km. (This perfectly preserved Maragatos village has heavily cobbled streets which are not conducive to cycling but is

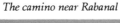

The camino near Rabanal

worth the visit.)

Return to the road (LE142) and begin a long steady climb, passing through a number of small villages - **Santa Catalina de Somoza** and **El Ganso** (each with its refuge and bar). The *camino* at this point takes the form of a shale track alongside the road. After leaving Astorga and travelling for 20km, enter the hillside village of **Rabanal** (refuges, hotel and bars).

DAY 30

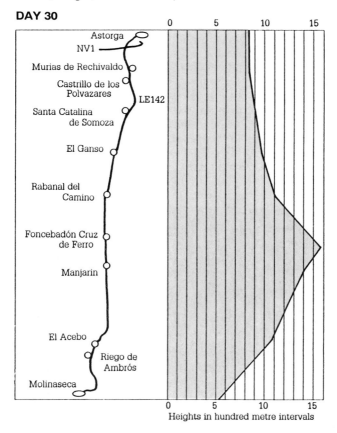

Heights in hundred metre intervals

N.B. The English refuge is closed until 4.00pm but the municipal refuge offers rest and refreshment for the weary pilgrim all day.

The climb over the Montes de León now begins in earnest on a well-surfaced road. After 5km, the abandoned village of **Foncebadón** appears to the left, but the road climbs on for another 3km to the **Cruz de Ferro** which is erected on a huge pile of stones left by pilgrims to signify the unloading of their sins. Do not assume that this mound marks the summit, however. This is 3km further on at an unmarked spot and even then the road dips and climbs several times before reaching the refuge at the abandoned village of **Manjarín**. (Here coffee and support are offered to all pilgrims who hear the summoning bell of Tomás, the warden.) From here, the road begins an ever steepening descent to Molinaseca, passing on the way the fascinating mountain village of **El Acebo** (bars). This, like other mountain hamlets, has the main road running through its centre but this road is not covered in smooth tarmac but slippery cobbles with a gutter running down its centre. On bicycles this is a potential death trap and extreme care should be taken, even in dry weather. Cyclists have died here. Be warned!

El Acebo - the main street

Molinaseca *with its refuge, hotels, restaurants, bars, shops and supermarket is a pretty village spanning the river. The Hostal El Palacio (Tel. 987.45.30.94) offers excellent accommodation.*

Day 31: Molinaseca to Villafranca del Bierzo (37km)

From **Molinaseca**, continue along the LE142 for **Ponferrada** (refuge, hotels, restaurants, bars, supermarket, shops including cycle repairs and bank). In 8km, this industrial town is reached. It is a very confusing place built on the side of a steep hill with mines and heavy industry abounding. The old part of the town with its castle of the Knights Templar is set to one side, up another hill to the left, and it is here that the refuge and the pilgrim office to stamp your Pilgrim Passport can be found.

The exit from Ponferrada is even more confusing. Road numbers have been changed and a distinct lack of directional signs serves to confuse matters. If in doubt, ask for help, but locals seem equally confused. At the roundabout below the castle, turn right and in 200m, turn left at traffic lights onto an arrow-straight road with the River Sil on your left which says N120 (but isn't). After 6km, take a road to the right immediately before the motorway. This route leads, on winding roads, through **Dehesas** and **Villaverde** (shop) to **Toral** (shops and bars). Turn right here onto the main road (N120) heading for (but not signed to) Villafranca del Bierzo.

Immediately before the NV1 passes over this road, take a turn to the left. This road runs parallel to the NV1, keeping it on your right. After 2km, enter a small village with an almost derelict bar on the left. Turn right beyond the bar, cross the defunct railway line and arrive, in 200m, at the NV1. Turn left onto this road and cycle the 5km into **Villafranca del Bierzo**.

This attractive little town is the best place to stay before the long climb up to O Cebreiro. It has a famous welcoming if rather basic refuge (Ave Fenix), several hotels (expensive), restaurants, bars, banks, supermarket and shops and cycle repairs. The church of Santiago has the Puerta del Perdón, where pilgrims who were too ill to continue could claim the same

DAY 31

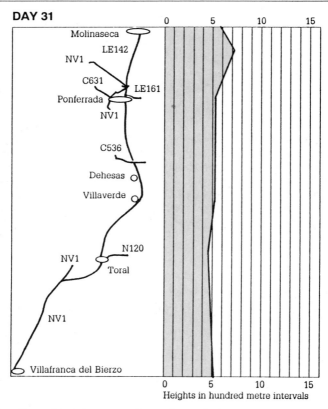

Heights in hundred metre intervals

benefits and indulgences as those who reached Santiago de Compostela.
There are several interesting churches and monasteries, some fine old
houses and a helpful tourist office. It is worth phoning the hostal *at O*
Cebreiro in order to try to book accommodation if you intend to stay there
at the end of the next leg. The tourist office will do this for you, using the
telephone at the bar next door!

Molanaseca. Pilgrims' bridge over the River Meruelo (Day 30)
Ponferrada. Thirteenth-century Templar Castle (Day 31)

Day 32: Villafranca del Bierzo to O Cebreiro (32km)

This is the longest climb on the whole pilgrimage but, because of this, it is not excessively steep until the col at Pedrafita is reached. In fact, much of the day's journey is similar, physically, to a hard day's ride in the English Lake District. Weather in this area is very unpredictable and you are advised to have plenty of warm, waterproof clothing available to wear at the summit, even in summer.

Leave **Villafranca del Bierzo** by riding through the main square and turning left to cross the first bridge. This is now the old NV1. Follow it to the second bridge but do not cross it. Instead, turn right and follow the road until it joins the new NV1 just beyond the badly lit road tunnel. Now turn right and follow the new NV1 for 12km. Here you should find a road signed to **Ambasmestas**. Take this. It is the old NV1 and from here it will take you on a delightful, quiet journey through mountain villages before meeting the new NV1 again at the col at Pedrafita.

Just 3km after leaving the new NV1, **Vega del Valcarce** (refuge, *pension*, bar and shops) will be reached. Keep straight on, climbing all the time and 2km later, **Ruitelán** with its chapel to San Froilán will be reached. A road to the left to La Faba should be ignored. Instead, watch in fascination as your road winds its way below the elevated section of the new road. It is hard to believe that you will climb to reach the road above but you will! Pass through **Castro** and watch out in about 1km for the T-junction with the new NV1. (This is just after the 'Welcome to Galicia' sign.)

Turn left onto the main road for 50m and (take care) turn left again at the **Pedrafita** sign onto the LU634, a road which climbs steeply out of the village, bearing slightly right as it does so. This road is steep and unrelenting for 5km and can be very exposed and daunting in bad weather which is often the case here. On reaching the Cebreiro altitude sign of 1,300m, turn left into the village of **O Cebreiro**.

Santiago de Compostela - The Cathedral

O Cebreiro is a unique village set high in the Cantabrian mountains. It has only about a dozen houses, half of which are ancient pallozas (strange thatched buildings dating back to the Bronze Age). There is a hostal, a refuge, a pension and a bar/restaurant. Do not miss the beautiful tiny church of Santa María and learn of its miracle.

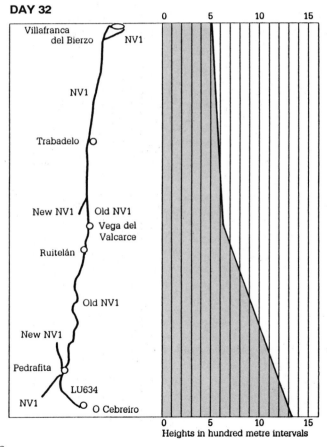

Heights in hundred metre intervals

Day 33: O Cebreiro to Sarria (48km)

Leave **O Cebreiro** by the LU634. After 4km of undulating riding with steep inclines, **Liñares** (shop, *hostal* and bar) will be reached. This is a possible overnight halt if there is no room available at O

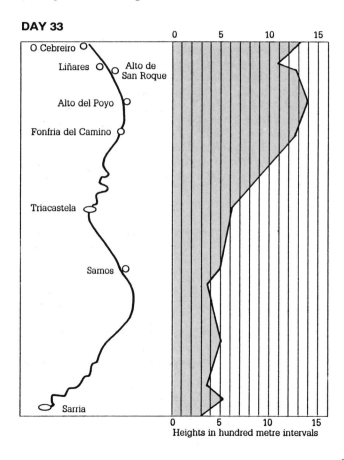

DAY 33

O Cebreiro
Liñares · Alto de San Roque
Alto del Poyo
Fonfria del Camino
Triacastela
Samos
Sarria

Heights in hundred metre intervals

Cebreiro. Ignore the LU651 to the left a kilometre later but continue to climb steadily as far as **Hospital de la Condesa** (refuge) in another 2km. The road now climbs steeply in a series of three sharp ascents for another 2km until the high point of **El Poyo** at 1,337m (hotel and bar/café for a well-earned rest) is reached. The weather along this stretch can be very severe, even in August, and care should be taken in high wind, low cloud and driving rain which can appear very suddenly.

From the summit, the road descends slowly and then begins an exciting descent of 12km to **Triacastela** (refuge, *hostal, fonda,* bars, restaurants, shops and supermarket; also see the church of Santiago.) The road surface is excellent with a large number of hairpin bends sweeping down the final 5km of descent. It is advised that halts are made every few kilometres to allow the rims to cool after excessive breaking. You will need no excuses to stop, though, as the views here are breathtaking.

The road climbs out of Triacastela for a short distance before following a wooded river valley for 11km into the pleasant small town of **Samos** (refuge, hotels, *hostal,* restaurants and bars). (The Benedictine monastery is worth a visit here - it also houses the refuge and has an extremely decorative stamp for your Pilgrim Passport.)

The road continues to wind its way in a series of climbs and swift descents through delightful, wooded scenery until, in 12km, it reaches **Sarria**.

This is a rather dreary town built chiefly along its main street. It has a refuge in the old town near the church of San Salvador up a stiff climb. There are a couple of hostales *(Hostal Londres, Tel. 53.24.56) and hotels. One is very expensive and the rest are only adequate if you are desperate for accommodation. You will find plenty of bars which serve food. There are also shops, supermarkets and banks. A cycle shop to the left at the entrance to the town is very helpful and likes to support pilgrims with quick, efficient and cheap service.*

Day 34: Sarria to Palas de Rei (53km)

Although the high mountains have been left behind for good, this is probably the hardest day's riding of the whole pilgrimage and should not be taken lightly. There are long stretches with nowhere to rest and a number of long ascents.

Leave **Sarria** (left at end of town) on the C535 signed for

DAY 34

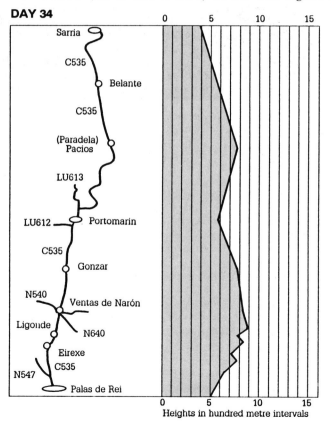

Heights in hundred metre intervals

Galician horreo *or grain store*

Portomarín. The road leaves by way of a very long, steep hill. Having crested this, one is then faced with a series of short, steep hills until **Pacios**, sometimes called **Paradela** (bars and shop) is reached after 15km.

The next 9km are one long, sweeping descent which brings you to the shores of a reservoir and the feet of the reconstructed town of **Portomarín** (refuge, *fonda*, rooms, restaurant, bars, shops and supermarket). This town was moved stone by stone from its original site in the river valley to escape flooding when the reservoir was constructed. Its rather perfect lay-out seems strange, as does its massively fortified church but a visit here is worth the very steep climb.

Exit the town down another steep hill before regaining the C535. A very long ascent follows with little shelter or shade until, in 13km, the N640 is met at **Ventas de Narón** (refuge, bar). This junction is complicated and it is essential you pick out the right road.

Do NOT turn right on the N640 (signed Lugo), but turn left and in 50 metres down the hill on the right (almost facing the refuge) you can see from the bridge over the N640. Take a road about 50m away, slightly to the left. This leads across country, through a number of tiny villages to your final destination for the day.

For the next 16km, the road switchbacks over delightful countryside, passing through **Prebisca, Lameiros, Ligonde, Eirexe** (refuge and bars), **Portos, Lestido, Valos, Brea** and **Rosario.** This road now meets the N547. If you wish, and have the strength to visit **Vilar de Donas** (Romanesque church), turn right here and take a road to the left after 3km. If not, turn left and climb steadily until the road leads you into the centre of **Palas de Rei.**

This unpretentious town has a refuge, fondas, *restaurants and bars as well as shops, banks and a supermarket. The Fonda Gundin has a beautiful new apartment block and the Casa Curro serves some of the best (and cheapest) meals on the* camino.

Day 35: Palas de Rei to Santiago de Compostela (73km)

Although the magnet of Santiago will be drawing you very strongly, it has to be said that whilst this road is well surfaced and has an excellent cycle track throughout its length, there are so many arduous hills on the route that you may feel an overnight stop at Monte del Gozo followed by an early morning ride into Santiago is more to your liking.

Descend on the main N547 (which you follow all day) bisecting **Palas de Rei** and ride through rolling countryside for 15km to **Melide** (refuge, hotels, *hostales,* restaurants, bars, shops and cycle repairs, supermarkets and banks). This is a busy town, particularly on market days.

From here to Santiago, do not expect to encounter any flat roads. Each hill is about 2km long and the descents are of a similar length. After 17km, **Arzua** (refuge, *fondas, hostales,* shops and cycle repairs, restaurants and bars) is reached. It has little to detain you, however, and Santiago is only another 35km away, or so the kilometre stones tell you.

The road now takes you through eucalyptus forests as it nears your destination. Bars along the side of the road become more frequent until, in about 18km, **Santiago airport** and the ancient settlement of **Labacolla** (*hostales* and bar) is reached. The people here seem unsympathetic to pilgrims and it is advised to move on to **Monte del Gozo** (refuge, bar and restaurant) which will be reached in 6km. The site of this enormous refuge is clearly signed to the left but it is unnecessary to visit it unless you are staying there as the famous first view of Santiago Cathedral is now obliterated by trees.

The road now plunges to cross the motorway. Keep straight on,

DAY 35

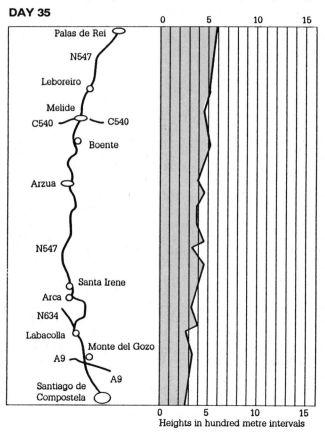

Heights in hundred metre intervals

always following signs for the town centre and the Cathedral (if in doubt bear right, keeping the bus station on your left). It is possible to ride straight into the Obradoiro square in front of the Cathedral.

Santiago de Compostela *has a large old quarter which has plenty of reasonably priced accommodation. There are many restaurants and bars as well as a tourist office, banks, shops, launderette, cycle repairs and supermarkets. The new part of the city is like any other large Spanish conurbation but the old quarter is worthy of several days' exploration. You should obtain your* Compostela *from the pilgrim office on the corner of the Rua do Villar and the Rua Gelmirez.*

You have arrived!

Santiago de Compostela

Many pilgrims leave Santiago feeling disappointed. They have travelled hundreds, sometimes thousands of miles to find a city teeming with non-pilgrim tourists sporting broom-handle staffs and plastic shells and gourds. What an anti-climax. But wait, there is more to this ancient city than that, though she is often shy to reveal her true treasures.

Most certainly, one cannot miss the Cathedral with its evocative sculptures, fine treasures and awe-inspiring botafumeiro filling its sanctuary with holy incense, but this is the tourist's domain and once the weary pilgrim has paid his respects to Saint James, one should decide to spend a few days in the city, teasing out its true beauty.

The best place to view the whole ancient quarter of Santiago is from the Carballeira de Santa Susana, a leafy park which used to be a fairground situated just beyond the Porta Faxeiras where the old town meets the new. An afternoon strolling here gives a totally new insight into this cosmopolitan city.

Another quiet sanctuary is the cloister of Santiago's University alongside the Plaza del Obradoiro. This portion of the university usually houses exhibitions, so entrance to it is rarely a problem. Sit and reflect here and you will soon be transported back to a time when scholars from all over the world were drawn here to study and marvel at the city's fine buildings.

In contrast, the Church of San Martiño Pinario will overwhelm you with its Baroque architecture both inside and out. Its interior, in particular, is so ornate as to stun the visitor into startled silence. Gilded cherubs dance exuberantly around blazing suns and the whole ensemble seems to have once adorned a fairground organ.

If you are looking for real life, however, head to the north-west of the city beyond the Puerta del Camino. Here you will discover the Convent of Santo Domingo de Bonaval. It is beyond the tourist zone and so it is rarely visited yet it houses two wonders. The first is an incredible triple spiral staircase similar in design to Da Vinci's at Chambord in France. The second and greater wonder, however, is the enormous and beautifully displayed museum of Galician life. It would be easy to spend a whole day here wandering from gallery to gallery, savouring the true nature of this north-west corner of Spain.

If you would like somewhere to sit and watch the world go by, why not use one of the benches in the Praza de Fonseca, one of the few tree-lined squares in the old city with its tinkling fountain only a stone's throw away from the bustling Praza do Obradoiro where street traders ply their wares and Japanese tourists photograph everything.

Finally, if you fancy some truly unashamed luxury, the Hostal de los Reyes Católicos can offer accommodation unrivalled the world over - at a price to take your breath away more rapidly than all the sights of Santiago put together.

Appendixes

A: USEFUL ADDRESSES

Confraternity of St. James,
First Floor,
1, Talbot Yard,
Borough High Street,
London SE1 1YP.

Cyclist Touring Club,
Cotterell House,
69, Meadrow, Godalming,
Surrey GU7 3HS.
Tel: 01483 417217

Gîtes d'étape
Gîtes de France Services,
56, rue St. Lazare,
75439 Paris, Cedex 09.
Tel: 01.49.70.75.75

Los Amigos del Camino de
    Santiago,
Apartado de Correos 20,
Estella, Navarra,
Spain.

European Bike Express,
31, Baker Street,
Middlesbrough,
Cleveland TS1 2LF.
Tel: 01642 251440

ALSA National Bus Company,
Estación Bus,
Santiago.
Tel: 981 58 61 33

Stanford's Map Shop,
12, Long Acre,
Covent Garden,
London WC2.
Tel: 0171 836 1321

The Map Shop,
15 High Street,
Upton-upon-Severn,
Worcs WR8 OHJ.
Tel: 01684 593 146

Dog-Dazer -
Richard Wiley,
43, Northcote Road,
London SW11 1YY.
Tel: 0171 228 2360

Cycle & Accessory Supplier -
Peter Handforth,
Wyre Wheels,
15b, Lower Green,
Poulton-le-Fylde,
Lancs. FY6 7JL.
Tel: 01253 896554

Camping Equipment & Clothing -
Cotswold,
42-46, Uxbridge Road,
Shepherd's Bush,
London W12 8ND.
Tel: 0181 743 2976

Cycle Manufacturer -
Trek U.S.A.,
15, Old Bridge Way,
Shefford,
Bedfordshire SG17 5HQ.
Tel: 01462 811458

Ortlieb Bags -
Lyon Equipment,
Rise Hill Mill,
Dent,
Sedbergh,
Cumbria LA10 5QL.

Coolmax Socks -
Ridgeview, Inc.
P.O. Box 8,
N.C. 28658.
U.S.A.
Tel: 001 704 464 2972

B: GLOSSARY OF TERMS

English	French	Spanish
accident	*un accident*	*el accidente*
bakery	*la boulangerie*	*la panadería*
bicycle	*la bicyclette*	*la bicicleta*
bottle	*la bouteille*	*la botella*
bridge	*le pont*	*el puente*
brake	*le frein*	*el freno*
broken	*s'éffondré*	*no funciona*
cable	*le câble*	*el cable*
castle	*le château*	*el castillo*
chain	*la chaîne*	*la cadena*
church	*l'église*	*la iglesia*
city	*la cité*	*la ciudad*
direction	*la direction*	*la dirección*
door	*la porte*	*la puerta*
field	*le champ*	*el campo*
garage	*le garage*	*el garaje*
gear	*la vitesse*	*el cambio*
grease	*la graisse*	*el lubricante*
handlebar	*le guidon*	*el manilla*
helmet	*le casque*	*el casco*
house	*la maison*	*la casa*
main road	*la route*	*la carretera*
map	*la carte*	*la mapa*
motorway	*l'autoroute*	*autopista/autovia*
nut	*l'écrou*	*la tuerca*
oil	*la huile*	*el aceite*
railway	*le chemin de fer*	*el ferrocarril*
river	*la rivière*	*el rio*
room	*la chambre*	*la habitación*
pass (mountain)	*le col*	*el puerto*
pedal	*la pédale*	*el pedal*
pilgrim	*le pèlerin*	*el peregrino*
pump	*la pompe*	*la bomba*
puncture	*la crevaison*	*el pinchazo*
saddle	*la selle*	*el asiento*
spanner	*la clé*	*la llave*
speed	*la vitesse*	*la velocidad*

spoke	*le rayon*	*el rayo*
square	*la place*	*la plaza/praza*
stamp (pilgrim)	*le tampon*	*el sello*
street	*la rue*	*la rùa/calle*
super(market)	*le (super)marché*	*el (super)mercado*
town hall	*l'hôtel de ville*	*el ayuntamiento*
tyre	*le pneu*	*el neumático*
way	*le chemin*	*el camino*
wheel	*la roue*	*la rueda*

C: BIBLIOGRAPHY

Hal Bishop, *The Way of St. James (The GR65)*. Milnthorpe, Cumbria: Cicerone, 1989.

A detailed guide for walkers covering the route between Le Puy in France and Roncesvalles in Spain, well illustrated, following the GR65 faithfully.

Alison Raju, *The Way of St. James (Spain)*. Milnthorpe, Cumbria: Cicerone, 1994.

A walker's guide to the Spanish section of the pilgrimage between Roncesvalles and Santiago de Compostela. It continues where Hal Bishop's guide left off. Replaced by guide to the entire route, 1998.

Alison Raju, *Le Puy to the Pyrenees*. London: The Confraternity of St. James, 1995.

A slim but extremely useful guide for the French section of the pilgrimage. There is much information about accommodation and meals.

Patricia Quaife, *Pilgrim Guide to Spain (Camino Francés)*. London: The Confraternity of St. James, 1997.

This guide, which is updated every year, has the most comprehensive information about places to eat and stay along the Spanish section of the pilgrimage route.

Bettina Selby, *Pilgrim's Road (A Journey to Santiago de Compostela)*. London: Abacus Travel, 1995.

An account of the author's journey by bicycle from Vézelay in France to Santiago de Compostela. The book is full of anecdotes regarding people and places she met on the way.

Michael Jacobs, *The Road to Santiago de Compostela (Architectural Guides for Travellers)*. London: Viking, 1990.

A comprehensive guide to the architecture the pilgrim will encounter on the way. It includes photographs, descriptions and plans of the historic treasures which have been built along the route to Santiago de Compostela.

Xavier Barral I Altet, *Compostelle - Le Grand Chemin*. France: Gallimard, 1993.

A beautifully illustrated and well-written account (in French) of the pilgrimage. Many of the photographs are in full colour and have been drawn from collections throughout the world.

Paulo Coelho, *The Pilgrimage*. San Francisco: Harper Collins, 1992.

A fictional account of the author's travels along the way on his quest to discover a magical sword.

Edward Mullins, *The Pilgrimage to Santiago*. London: Secker & Warberg, 1974.

A description of all aspects of the pilgrimage route between Paris and Santiago de Compostela.

Rob Neillands, *The Road to Compostela*. Ashbourne: Moorland Publishing, 1985.

This is an account of a journey made by the author from Le Puy to Santiago. It gives a lasting impression of the flavour of the journey.

Dr. Elias Valiña Sampedro, *The Pilgrim's Guide to the Camino de Santiago*. Vigo: Editorial Galaxia, 1992.

A full guide to the Spanish section of the pilgrimage by the man who spent his life promoting it. Well illustrated with maps and photographs.

James Hogarth, *A XIIc Pilgrim's Guide (A Translation)*. London: The Confraternity of St. James, 1992.

Translated from the Latin, this gives a fascinating insight into the world of the twelfth-century traveller.

Hubert de Torcy, *Carnet de Route pour Compostelle*. France: Le Sarment Fayard, 1995.

Written in French by a twenty-two year old, this account gives a vivid insight into the spiritual dimensions of Pilgrimage.

Dr. Elias Valiña Sampedro, *The Way of St. James (The Pilgrimage Route to Santiago de Compostela)*. Brentford: Roger Lascelles, 1993

A book of hand-drawn maps of the Spanish section of the pilgrimage by the man who revived interest in it.

Annick & Serge Mouraret, *Gîtes d'étape, Refuges, France et Frontières*. Vélizy: La Cadole, 1996.

A complete list of *gîtes d'étape* throughout France with telephone numbers and brief descriptions.